Secrets

of

GREATNESS

Advice from the World's
Top CEO's and Entrepreneurs

by the Editors of **FORTUNE**

Published by
Fortune Books

Time Inc.
135 West 50th Street, 10th Floor
New York, N.Y. 10020

ISBN 13: 978-1-933405-90-2
ISBN 10: 1-933405-90-2

Special thanks to: Eric Pooley, Hank Gilman, Ellyn Spragins, Dan Goodgame, Josh Quittner, Gene Foca, Matthew Hoffmeyer, Robert Newman, Carrie Welch, Susan Williams, Marilyn Adamo, Peter Harper, Chavaughn Raines and Michelle Gallero.

For bulk orders, please call 1-212-522-8282

For single copy orders, please call 1-800-327-6388
CENTRAL TIME: Monday - Friday 7:00 AM - 8:00 PM and Saturday 7:00 AM -6:00 PM

TABLE OF CONTENTS

I. GREAT BEGINNINGS

How Some of America's Best-Known Entrepreneurs Got Started

II. GREAT WAYS TO WORK

Techniques and Tips From The Masters

III. GREAT DECISIONS
Making the Right Choice at the Right Time

IV. GREAT ROLE MODELS:
Let Leaders Who Break the Mold Be Your Inspiration

V. GREAT TEAMS:
How the Best Make It Happen

VI. GREAT ADVICE:
Words That Made a Difference to the World's Best Managers

A RANDOM WALK:
ONE MAN'S EVOLUTION INTO LEADERSHIP

By Andy Grove

As I read through this collection of varied and rich stories of management and managers, I reflected on my own development as a manager. Try as I might, I could not get away from the thought that it took place by a process often called a random walk. Random walk is a mathematical term, often illustrated by the description of an inebriated person walking in the forest, bumping into a tree and setting out again until the next bump. I became a manager bump to bump. Sometimes the bump was so strong I staggered afterwards, but each time my stride got more confident and my direction more steady.

The first of these bumps had to do with my role in saving a good employee from being laid off a few days after I was named supervisor, at a company called Fairchild Semiconductor in the 1960s. The person in question did not work for me, and when I appealed on behalf of this individual, my boss made me a simple proposal. "You can save him, and have him, if you lay off one of the members of the department." I gritted my teeth and did just that. This was two days after I had been named a boss. The reality hit: as a boss, I would be called upon to make decisions affecting the lives of other people. No one told me that when they congratulated me on my promotion. Dealing with this horrible choice tore me up, as did many similar choices I would have to make in a career spanning forty-some years.

Before long I started to read about what managers are supposed to do. In most texts, the role was summarized in the succinct phrase, "Plan-Organize-Control." The words rang hollow.

I didn't plan, I reacted. At first I reacted to what my boss told me to do. Later on, I reacted to moves by competitors or to changes in technology. I rarely organized anything. My activities were better characterized by incessant follow-up on things people promised me and didn't do—or things they should have promised me but I forgot to ask for.

And control? The word "nudge" or "cajole" would better describe what I most often have done through the years. As I got to be a higher and higher level manager, the only thing that changed was that I got to nudge and cajole higher and higher level people upon whom my success depended. This was just as well. Being a freshly minted Ph.D. in the 1960s, I thought the idea of "control" sounded vaguely sinister. What was I, a drill sergeant or a Nazi? I was so hesitant to look like I was giving orders that one of my subordinates actually pulled me aside and informed me that it was okay with him if I told him what to do.

So how would I characterize being a manager if Plan-Organize-Control is not an accurate description? Another bump—although not a painful one—tells the story. I was a young father of small children and sometimes I had the chance to read them their bedtime stories. One of them was the story of the Old Testament, written in a conversational style. The part that described Joseph's story characterized him in such a memorable way that it has shaped my concept of what a manager should be for decades. As I recall, the story said that Joseph was cherished and respected because he always had "time for people". This rang true to me. I had discovered that people turned to me for advice or to convince me of their particular point of view. Listening to them was very time-consuming. But I found that when I made time for a person, both of us finished with a better understanding of each other and the issue at hand. So I tried to be like Joseph in the story.

As I accumulated experience as a manager, I stumbled on other excruciating responsibilities. Being the one to find, tell and act on unpleasant truths was one of these. Some of the most important actions of my managerial career were defined by facing unpleasant truths. On one occasion, described in business school cases and in my own recollections, I realized that our company, Intel, had lost its ability to participate in the business it was founded for—to build memory chips. If there was a mouse hole in which I could have hid from this reality, I would have. It was a hard truth because our identity was tied up with memory chips. And because it was hard to face, we acted on this realization tentatively and with reluctance. But the truth ultimately forced us to do what we had to. What made it particularly agonizing was the need to choose who stayed and who would go in the new order. Like my first bump in the forest, this was agonizing. But the truth pursues you.

Once Intel grew to be a big company I could no longer reach out and touch most of our employees—or even most of our managers. Yet at times it was necessary for me to touch their brains, as well as their hearts—the source of their innate drive. Focusing on a particularly critical product transition, the move to the first Pentium processor, was such a task. I wished I could buttonhole every manager and employee to explain why nothing they might do was as important to the future of the company as that product launch. I couldn't talk to each one, so I summed the argument into a two-word slogan: "Job One." I applied all my energy to drumming the Job One beat ad nauseam, until people understood that unless they worked on the Pentium ramp, they were working on the second or third most important task in the company.

This experience introduced me to a vital skill that people in charge of big organizations have to perfect: reaching people you don't know over large distances with complex messages. The task of communicating one-to-many at a distance—as contrasted with one-to-one by direct contact-defines leadership to me far more appropriately than most of the psychobabble that I have read and listened to in lectures and articles. Communicating in this way sounds simpler than it is. You must distill complex thoughts into phrases that cross great distances and mean the same thing to people with varied experiences. Think of Churchill, Roosevelt or President Kennedy. Often the first thing that comes to mind is a few of their carefully crafted phrases.

Of course, we are not born with this skill, any more than we're born with the skill of nudging. We learn it. There are lots of opportunities to learn because such communication is particularly needed at times of crisis. Crises are just more bump-producing trees in the dark forest. While the pain of encountering each remains as sharp as ever, a key management trait is that I've learned to pick myself up more quickly afterward.

There is a particularly insidious trap in the managerial forest that comes out and grabs you when you least expect it. These traps are hidden assumptions. When you formulate a decision or a strategy on the basis of such an assumption, you build on quicksand. One of the reasons we at Intel hung on to our business of building memory chips long after we stopped being a significant provider was our conviction that being in this business was necessary for developing process technology for other kinds of chips as well. As events later proved, this assumption-because that's what it was—was wrong, but we had a very hard time overcoming its gravitational pull. Mark Twain understood this when he said, "It ain't what you don't know that gets you into trouble. It's what you know for sure that just ain't so."

Sometimes these assumptions come in the form of truisms. For example, it's often said that one of the mistakes organizations make is to promote their best individual performers into management. The thinking goes: You stupid fool, in doing that you not only lost your best individual performer, you gained a bumbling manager. I learned to question the obviousness of this assumption. Should you have done the opposite and promoted

8

your worst individual performer, and let him or her pass judgment on more competent people? What would you be communicating to the multitudes of other engineers about your values if you rewarded someone they considered an incompetent engineer? When Apple ran their memorable advertising campaign, exhorting customers to "Think Different," I think they were talking about avoiding the trap of hidden assumptions.

How does a manager work his way through this forest faster? I learned through many smaller knocks in the head that there is a very simple tool to move faster, to increase productivity. It has to do with the things you decide not to do. The most important two letters that increase your productivity as well as the productivity of the people you work with are N-O, said clearly, unequivocally and early-not after somebody has decided to count on you.

An important example is declining to participate in meetings that you have been invited to. Maybe you were invited because people didn't want to offend you by not including you. Maybe you were invited because historically you used to be a participant. Everybody labors, you attend a meeting you are no longer needed in, and they bend over backwards to include you, all for no good reason. It is so much simpler and more productive to say, "I no longer need to or plan to attend."

Why is it so hard to say no? I haven't figured it out. But the number of phone calls, e-mails, letters and applications that go unanswered every day in our enlightened industrial/technological society is evidence that for whatever reason it is difficult to say no.

There's a lot of handwringing these days about the need for ethics in business-and the role of managers to communicate the value of ethical behavior. But how do you decide what is ethical? Many years ago I developed a test that, like a canary warning the miners of the presence of poison gases, alerted me if I was considering shaky conduct. This is how it worked. In those days

I routinely spoke to large groups of new employees as part of their orientation process. The new employees regularly peppered me with questions about any and all subjects. If the prospect of answering questions about a contemplated course of action—a reorganization, a change in employee benefits, a new workplace rule, whatever—gave me some discomfort, I took that as a sign that something was wrong with what we were planning to do. Nowadays, I would supplement this test by asking myself how comfortable I would be explaining the contemplated action on the The Daily Show with Jon Stewart. It amounts to the same thing.

It's been a long walk through the forest of being a manager-40 years long in fact. The trees continue to emerge from the dark. The good news is, my forehead is stronger than it was 40 years ago. Perhaps reading the stories that follow and applying them to your situation may save you a bump or two on the head.

FOREWORD

By Eric Pooley

You know that feeling you get—a surge of exhilaration, tinged with alarm—after you land a new job and you're sprinting to keep up with its demands? You're handling everything, dashing along the track, when it occurs to you that this isn't a sprint; it's a marathon. How are you going to sustain this pace?

I was feeling that way in the spring of 2005, after I became managing editor of Fortune*—a job with a lot of parts, some of which required me to stretch in new ways. Soon after I got the position, the CEO of a major Wall Street investment bank invited me to an off-the-record, one-on-one dinner. We met in an out-of-the-way Manhattan restaurant and talked for hours. I was eager to discover how the world looked to him, and he was happy to share his views on the rocky markets and the burgeoning trade deficit and the flat, shrinking world. But he really came alive when I asked him the most basic question of the evening: "How do you work?"*

It was a simple question with a complex answer, because his job was so demanding: assessing risk and allocating capital, seeing around corners to anticipate the next crisis, managing the endless flood of information, communicating with his global workforce and driving his strategic vision across a huge company. But he wasn't sprinting; he was flowing smoothly through his marathon days. And he'd worked out all sorts of ways to boost his effectiveness. "I hate email," he told me at one point. "I try not to use it for anything that really matters. Emails are just too easy for people to misinterpret - and too easy for people to forward. I'd rather leave a long voicemail message explaining exactly what I think, so the person on the receiving end doesn't have to read between the lines. One of the keys to leadership is clarity."

As I met with other business leaders in the months that followed, I found that all of them had developed secret strategies for coping with their impossibly demanding jobs. That wasn't surprising—if they hadn't, they wouldn't have lasted. But here's what I didn't expect: Those personal strategies turned out to be incredibly useful to me as I learned to cope with my own demanding job. And it required no great leap to imagine that my Fortune *readers - most of them up to their necks in work and trying to lead others, just like I was - might find this material as relevant as I did.*

So was born a Fortune *special issue called "How I Work," in which a dozen superacheivers shared their tools for success. It became the first in a series we called* Secrets of Greatness, *and the response from our readers was overwhelming—so strong, in fact, and so sustained as we continued the* Secrets of Greatness *series, that we decided to collect the best advice from our pages and put it all between the covers of this book.*

Fortune *has always been in the business of taking readers inside the mind of the world's best managers, and issues such as "How to Become a Great Leader" (featuring Andy Grove), "The Best Advice I Ever Got" (featuring Warren Buffett) and "How to Make Great Decisions" (featuring Jim Collins) have proved to be some of our most popular. You'll find all of those stories here, along with terrific, usable lessons drawn from our sister publications* Fortune Small Business *and* Business 2.0. *Whether you're an entrepreneur launching your first start-up, a small business owner trying to scale up, a manager running a division or the boss of a global company, you'll find great takeaway here: hard-won, field-tested stuff that works. And I think you'll experience the same happy shock of recognition I did when sitting across from that master investment banker in the spring of 2005. Hey, his challenges aren't so different from mine. I'm going to test drive some of his solutions.*

Enjoy the ride.

ERIC POOLEY
Managing Editor, *Fortune*

Great
BEGINNINGS

*How Some of America's
Best-Known Entrepreneurs Got Started*

GREAT BEGINNINGS

*How Some of America's
Best-Known Entrepreneurs Got Started*

One day you're scrubbing in the shower or driving in your car—whatever you do to kill time between episodes of *The Anna Nicole Show*—and suddenly a notion takes shape in your brain. Before you know it, it's pointing you toward a destiny you know better than to try to escape. Finally you understand what you were born to do. Just make sure your mission doesn't involve starting your own business, because, quite simply, entrepreneurial success doesn't happen that way.

Yes, everybody assumes that the fellow who started FedEx or the woman who helped create the PalmPilot had the same kind of fleeting notion that most of us have now and then—"Gee, wouldn't it be great to have a store where people could load up on a month's worth of correction fluid at once?" But the difference between these folks and the rest of us is that they had the guts to act on their dream rather than just sit around. That doesn't mean, however, that these entrepreneurs act impulsively. In fact, they actually take their time, learning about and analyzing their products and markets before making a move. How do we know? Well, we asked them not only to tell us how they created or re-created entire industries but also to put the experience into their own words. What these founders decided to share—not just individually but collectively—had little to do with crushing insights or burning cravings.

Viewed up close, the much-vaunted "eureka moment" isn't a moment at all; it's a stretch of time that begins, and ends, with an intense focus on learning. In the middle, these industry-changing entrepreneurs act with speed but not haste. They detect a pattern, make a move, then assess what they've achieved before forging on. They live at the intersection of thought and action, where they somehow manage to think deeply without becoming paralyzed.

—*Joshua Hyatt*

SOFTWARE BY THE NUMBERS

By Scott Cook

When Scott Cook was trying to decide whether to take up entrepreneurship, he surveyed hundreds of people who had started their own businesses. Their advice: If he decided to do it, he should fashion himself into an industry—inverting visionary. Okay, so it didn't quite happen that way. But with Cook, who in 1983 co-founded software giant Intuit, it seems that just about every eureka moment he's had has been buttressed by rigorous testing. Such meticulousness reflects Cook's training: He spent several years as a marketer at Procter & Gamble, where "they taught us to understand the customer."

Determined that Intuit, now a $2 billion publicly held business, would follow that principle, Cook didn't act on his original hunches until he had talked to hundreds of potential customers. That research convinced him that there was indeed a market for money-management software, provided it was streamlined and simple instead of loaded with complex features. How right was he? By 1994, Intuit was poised to merge with Microsoft, a marriage the Justice Department ultimately scuttled. "I thought it would be exciting in some ways, but I probably wouldn't be with the combined company now had that happened," Cook says. "Founders have not done well when acquired by big, centralized companies like Microsoft."

Of course, Intuit itself has become a giant company, and Cook has adjusted his role accordingly, bringing in an outside CEO in 1994. "I recognized my skill set was holding the company back," says Cook, now chairman of Intuit's executive committee. To this day, he remains a believer in the all-too-rare art of listening. "It's amazing what people will tell you," he muses. What's equally amazing is what Cook has created by hearing them. —JOSHUA HYATT

I would describe the start of Intuit as more of a eureka insight than a moment. The moment is really just the beginning of a journey and, in fact, only a way station on that journey. But the centerpiece of it is an insight that challenges the common wisdom. It's when you implement that that you end up revolutionizing an industry.

Most of our major businesses at Intuit are based on a eureka insight. Quicken was the first of those. It really came from two separate insights at two separate times. The first was when my wife complained about doing the bills, and it was her complaining about the bills that caused me to say, "Ding! This would be a great use for the computer." I thought that because of the inherent nature of the work and the inherent set of things that computers are good at. However, that was not a unique insight. There were a lot of other people who thought computers might be good for doing personal finance. In fact, when we launched Quicken there were roughly 25 other personal-finance products on the market. So the idea of using a computer to do finances was not novel, even in the very early days.

I had always toyed with starting a business. When I was in junior high I sold Christmas cards door-to-door to earn money. And in high school I looked at going into the cuff-link business. In college, at the University of Southern California, I ended up running a club that was really more like a business. In two years I took the ski club from having no leader and being bankrupt to being the largest campus organization at the university. When I was a consultant [at Bain], I toyed with the idea of going into the windsurfing travel business. With a buddy of mine, we ran the first—to my knowledge—windsurfing package tour in the U.S. It was a great success. But it was not a business that appealed to me. It looked as if it would remain a boutiquey, small, custom business.

At about the same time, though, I listened to my wife's complaints about doing the bills. So the first of the two eureka insights was "Oh, wow, this is a good use of a computer." Computers could do this job well, whereas a lot of jobs that people were alleging computers would do well, they were actually poor at doing. Storing recipes was a truly stupid use of a computer. There were a lot of really bad ideas proposed for the use of computers by people who were non-insightful. What are computers best at? Numbers and data storage. And finance is all about numbers and storage, plus there's a high degree of repetition. The bills you pay go to the same people every month, in general. So once you've typed it in, you don't have to retype it.

But having the insight that finance is a good use for a computer was not the key to success. The key was the second insight I had, which came about from surveying customers. I got the phone book, called up households, and tried to understand what they did in their finances—their likes and their dislikes. I picked mostly upscale neighborhoods, the kinds I thought would have computers at the time, which was 1982. And the insight that came out of that was that people weren't turned on by doing graphs or other fancy stuff. They just wanted to get the work done, and they wanted to do it as quickly and easily as possible.

> "I WOULD DESCRIBE THE START OF INTUIT AS MORE OF A EUREKA INSIGHT THAN A MOMENT,"
>
> —SCOTT COOK, *founder of Intuit.*

None of the software products on the market were designed to do that. They offered a huge amount of complexity, rather than being optimized for speed and ease. There was a whole belief that the more features you had, the better. The industry paradigm was wrong for this segment, for this purpose, for what customers wanted in personal finance.

Yet the products in the market did sell. In fact, the most complex ones actually tended to sell better. This seemed incongruous; something didn't fit. So the only way I could get to the bottom of that was to actually interview customers who were using the personal-finance software products. The companies in the industry wouldn't give me their names, of course. So I wound up calling people in the computer industry to find those who had tried personal-finance software. I called computer stores and I called people at computer magazines. Sixty-five percent of those in the computer industry whom I interviewed had tried personal-finance software. And 61 percent had tried it and quit. I asked, "Why did you quit?" And the answer was "It was too slow, too hard."

So we made Quicken fast and easy. The catch is, if you're going to make it fast and easy, it's got to be fast and easy in the hands of the customer, not in my hands or an engineer's hands. We were the first to do usability testing of any kind of PC software. We would just bring in people and have them use prototypes. We didn't tell them how to use it. We just watched. And that would tell us what wasn't working, what wasn't obvious. Then we'd go back and fix it, and then retest it. It's that second insight that made Quicken dramatically different from the other competitors, which is why it became huge and the other ones have died.

But we almost failed twice. When we went out to get venture capital, in the first half of 1984, we totally struck out. We were looking for $2 million. I couldn't get anyone interested because we flew against the entire paradigm set. First of all, they didn't believe that consumers would buy computers. Second, even if someone believed consumers would buy computers, they didn't believe that consumers would do their finances on computers. Third, even if you got someone who could believe those two things, no one believed they would do their finances with us, because they believed that having more features was the key to success.

Here we were, doing a simple version. And the investors couldn't point to anyone who had succeeded with our strategy. Every one of them passed. But that's what typically happens if something is truly a major eureka. It means it's a different mind-set—not merely an extrapolation of what other people have already done. So most people think it's wrong, or if they don't think it's wrong, they think it's unimportant. That's why we couldn't raise any money. By this point I had spent all the money I'd saved. All totaled, with the money from my parents, we'd gone through about $360,000.

One of the guys in the company said, "Hey, it's clear this VC thing isn't working. Let's go talk to some rich people." I didn't know any rich people. But he knew two. We went and talked to them together. We got $151,000, and that kept the doors open for another six months. Then we almost went out of business a second time. We'd been selling Quicken to banks, which would resell it to their customers. After we sold to the first two banks, we ran out of money. We had to stop paying salaries. And it became clear that banks couldn't sell the software. There went our sales channel, and half of our people had left, three out of seven. They had to find jobs that actually paid money. That was in 1986. We finally put everything we had into selling at retail, and fortunately that worked.

I contacted a friend whom I'd met in the industry. He went and personally sold to the first distributor. It was a very small distributor, and because of this personal relationship my friend got him to accept it. Then I found out that a guy who had once tried to hire me was now the head of sales for a distributor. He knew I did good stuff. So he stuck it in their catalog. Then it was my job to create demand. Word of mouth turns out to be the best way to do that. And it worked for us.

Today Quicken is just 5 percent to 7 percent of our total revenue. The rest comes from other eureka insights. One came out of another quandary. We sold Quicken, and we were surveying our customers, and one of the questions was "Do you use Quicken in the home or business or both?" It turned out that half the customers used it in business. At first we ignored that. Another year and a half went by. By 1988 we had a couple more surveys that showed the same thing. It finally dawned on me to ask, "What's going on?"

So I called up some of the businesses and asked, "What are you doing? Why are you using this instead of using accounting software that was specifically designed for business?" Based on those results we did a randomized set of calls to small businesses—in other words, not just to our customers. The eureka insight we got from that was that if you have a company of 15 people, you don't have room on the payroll for a trained accountant. So the person who keeps the books is somebody else—it could be the owner, the owner's spouse, the office manager. And the vast majority of these people don't know debits and credits, and don't want to learn. So we actually built a product for businesses.

"WHEN YOU DO SOMETHING TRULY REVOLUTIONARY, MOST COMPETITORS WILL NEVER COPY IT—THEY WON'T EVEN UNDERSTAND IT."

After two years of development, we launched QuickBooks in March 1992. Just four months after launch, we got data that showed that QuickBooks had become the clear market leader. When you do something that's truly revolutionary, something that's truly one of those major paradigm shifts that come from eureka insights, it delivers as long as you execute really well. Most of the competitors will never copy it—they won't even understand it—and they'll go out of business. The eureka insight can be that powerful. And this company is still a place where people who have eureka insights can make big change happen. We have a tradition of eureka here.

BUILDING THE PERFECT MACHINE

By Michael Dell

W hen Michael Dell was just a high school student in Dallas, he came across the product that would change his life: the personal computer. While his peers tossed footballs and swigged beer, Dell started the business that would lead him to fame and fortune two decades later. The young Dell started buying his own computer parts, assembling cheap machines, and selling them to his classmates. He made a pass at college but dropped out of the University of Texas after freshman year to officially launch his company: Dell Computer. More than 20 years later Dell remains chairman of his firm, which in 2006 posted sales of $56 billion and employed 69,700 people. Michael Dell's success has made him a legend in his own time: He has revolutionized the computer industry, proved that e-commerce isn't always a dirty word, and built a small empire, all before his 40th birthday. How has Dell been able to maintain fast growth and steal market share? The company has a unique business model: It builds a computer only after a customer orders one. That keeps inventory costs down, allowing Dell to undersell the competition. The company also keeps close tabs on the market. By dealing directly with the customer either by phone or online, Dell gathers valuable data on purchasing habits that allow it to quickly change its products and services. Says Dell: "One of the great things about our business is we have immediate information. We don't have to wait a week or a month or until the end of a quarter for information. We get information about our customers every single day." That's proved to be a tough business model to beat. Here's his story. —BRIAN DUMAINE

My parents first sparked my interest in business. We lived in Houston. My mother was a financial advisor and my father an orthodontist. When I was a kid in the 1970s, we'd sit around the dinner table talking about inflation, the oil crisis—that sort of thing. When I was a second-grader I started my first business, selling candy. In third grade I applied in the mail for a high school equivalency degree. I saw this thing in the back of a magazine, and I thought, "I'll try that.'" A few weeks later this woman knocked on the door and said, "Is Mr. Michael Dell there?" And my mother said, "What is this in regards to?" And the woman said, "We're from the so-and-so company, and we'd like to talk to him about high school equivalency." And my mother said, "Well, he's taking a bath right now, but I'll get him." So I came out in my little red bathrobe. As soon as the saleswoman saw me, she decided that was the end of her sales pitch.

A few years after that I created a stamp-auction business. And it was kind of a direct-mail thing, where I was getting people who wanted to consign stamps together with people who wanted to sell stamps, and then getting them to bid on stamps.

In high school I bought myself an Apple II computer, which was the PC of choice at the time. I took it apart, learned about how it worked, what was inside, and how to upgrade the machine. That kicked off my whole interest in computers. I set up a bulletin board system, and I was upgrading computers and reselling them at a profit to my friends.

When I was 16, I had a summer job doing phone sales at the *Houston Post*. And they gave me a big long list of phone numbers to call and say, "Hey, I'm from the *Houston Post*. How'd you like to buy the newspaper?" I soon realized that there were two kinds of people who were buying newspapers: people who had just moved and people who had just gotten married. That seemed logical enough. So then I asked, "Is there any way I can find all these people who are getting married or have just moved?"

And it turns out that in the state of Texas, when you get married you have to apply for a marriage license. When you apply for a marriage license, you put an address of where you want the license sent. And that's usually where you're going to live. So it's not that hard to figure out what to do next: Go to all the counties in the surrounding area, start gathering up all these names of people, and send them direct-mail offers. All of a sudden I had thousands and thousands of people who wanted to buy the newspaper. I made $18,000 in commissions and went out and bought more computers. I bought a car, stereos, basically anything a 16-year-old would want.

Then I went off to the University of Texas to be premed. My freshman year I started selling computers out of my dorm room. I was doing what I had done in high school, but my parents weren't around to force me to study, so I could do a lot more of it. As I got further into this computer stuff, I realized that the industry was incredibly inefficient. There were dealers like the now-defunct ComputerLand that bought from manufacturers or distributors and then sold the machines to the public. When you opened up a $2,000 PC, you'd find only about $600 worth of parts inside of it.

> "I SAID TO MYSELF, 'IF I CAN MAKE $80,000 SELLING FROM MY APARTMENT, I CAN PROBABLY DO $1 MILLION A MONTH WITH AN OFFICE AND A TIE.'"

And it took about a year from the time the part was available till the time it actually got to the customer. That meant that your computer, to put it kindly, wasn't the latest technology—if you want to be extreme, you could say it was obsolete. I would read in the industry publications that Intel had this new superfast processor, but the best one that I could buy in the store was only half that speed. It was just gross inefficiency in the inventory and supply chain.

In May of '84, I dropped out of college and set up in a 1,000-square-foot office in Austin. At that time PCs didn't come with hard drives. But you could put together a kit to upgrade a computer with a hard drive. That's how the company got started, selling upgrade kits for computers.

And from there, we just kept growing. The funny thing is,

there really wasn't one moment when the idea for the business came to me. It was a little more pragmatic and incremental than that. It doesn't sound like a story made for television, but it's true. I said to myself, "If I can make $80,000 selling computers from my apartment, I can probably do $1 million a month with an office and a tie."

We lasted only about a month in that office and then needed 2,500 square feet. We lasted about three months there, and then we moved to a larger space, with 7,000 square feet. We were like gypsies, always moving to bigger and bigger offices.

So we were growing, but I didn't have any capital, and I had to do a number of things to fund the business. I had customers paying by credit card when we shipped. I had wire transfers of money going back and forth. I had suppliers who would say, "Well, I don't really know if you're going to be in business, but I don't have many customers, so I'll give you some credit." And I would figure out how to make it work.

We screwed up all kinds of things, but there was so much inherent value in what we were doing that it masked all the mistakes that we made. Still, we didn't make a lot of the same mistakes over and over again. We learned from the mistakes and figured out how we could progress.

Even when we made mistakes, though, we kept to our core principles. From the beginning, there was definitely an ethic around the customers: How do we serve the customers? There was a philosophy in the company that we're going to do what's right, which is how my parents taught me to treat people as well as customers.

It was easy to communicate that philosophy. For the first couple of years, everything was all right there in one place. So we just spread our values through our actions every day. For example, you could be doing your job, and somebody would come in and say, "Hey, what do we do about this problem this customer had?" That right there defines the philosophy of the company: We'll do whatever we have to do to get this customer happy.

But that doesn't mean you should give every customer

everything he wants. You have to consider first of all what the customer is willing to pay for. If I say, "I want seven-by-24 support, I want one-hour service, I want this and that," am I willing to pay for all that? Because those things aren't free. Today we have a lot of tiered services. We have gold service and silver service and platinum service—a customer picks what he wants.

Our management, though, is not tiered. From the beginning, we've tried to create a management structure that doesn't have a lot of layers. This means first of all understanding the business model, being result-oriented, being speedy, and setting aggressive goals. It also means being self-critical and willing to talk about problems openly. For example, let's say somebody knows that there's a problem but he comes to a meeting and tries to pretend there isn't one. We just tell him right there in the meeting, "That's not going to work." The organization has such a well-honed culture at this point that if somebody shows up and doesn't drive for results and try to eliminate bureaucracy, the organization bypasses him. We're not going to pay attention to that person.

In the early days I found it helpful to have a board of directors, especially when we got into problems. Even when things were going well, the members would tell us what to watch out for. But they really helped us when we got into new territory and didn't know what we were doing. They helped us avoid problems that might otherwise have been very dangerous.

For instance, when we were about a $2 million or $3 million company, we had challenges with our financial controls. One board member, Don Carty, who was an executive vice president of American Airlines, knew infinitely more about this than we did. He spent time with us and helped us distill a culture of financial controls from an auditing standpoint that was extremely helpful.

We had to make cultural shifts too. In the early '90s we took a foray into retailing. That was a mistake. At the time the conventional wisdom was that direct sales was only a niche market, and we believed that. Then these wholesale warehouse clubs emerged, what became CompUSA and Sam's Club. It wasn't quite the dealer channel, it wasn't quite direct. And we said,

"Why don't we try this? It will be a great way for us to get to the consumer." But it kind of violated a lot of the principles that had helped the company succeed. It destroyed the integrity of the customer relationship that Dell is really based on. The relationship became one between the store and the customer. Fortunately, it never became a very big part of the business, so we were able to shut it off quickly. One of the great things about our culture is that it's so used to changing and adjusting. You can say, "Okay, now we're going to go do the Internet, now we're going to do servers, now we're going to do services." People are preconditioned for change.

"WHY HAVE I SURVIVED ALL THESE YEARS? FIRST OF ALL, I'M HAVING FUN."

—MICHAEL DELL, *Dell Computer*

Why have I survived all these years? One, I'm having fun. Two, I think I've always approached my job by asking what the company needs to be successful. Whatever it is, I'm going to do it. And that means I have to change. For instance, we have a 360 process inside our company where employees are evaluated by those above and below them. I stood up before our executive team a few months ago and said, "Here's my 36—here's what I'm working on improving." The important message for our team was we all have to improve and we're all going to improve. And this is serious stuff. When we talk about growing new elements of our business, you can't say, "I've been here ten years, so I don't have to do that."

A NEW TWIST ON TIMELESS TOYS

By Pleasant Rowland

Some might say that 45 is too old to be playing with dolls, but for Pleasant Rowland it was the beginning of something historic. Rowland's midlife foray into the business of posable arms and tiny shoes made her not only a hero to little girls nationwide but a toy-industry legend. When Rowland debuted her American Girl dolls in 1986, the industry pegged her eponymous Pleasant Company as a surefire failure. Everyone knew, of course, that many girls abandon doll play after age 6. A line of historical dolls for 7- to 12-year-olds? Preteen girls had largely been ignored as a distinct demographic—and they turned out to be a multibillion-dollar opportunity. With 82 million books and seven million dolls, the American Girl line is second only to Barbie as the most popular doll in America. Their 2001 sales: $350 million. But Rowland insists it is the books that unlock the mystery of American Girl's staggering success. Each of the eight American Girl dolls has a series of six books that tell her life story. Felicity's details life in Colonial America; Kit's teaches girls the lessons of growing up during the Depression. Along with the books, the dolls have a universe of extras like matching outfits for doll and owner, mini tea sets and steamer trunks to enact scenes from the books, and American Girl magazine, with 650,000 subscribers. "Chocolate cake with vitamins" is how Rowland describes the mix of imagination, history, and values. She holds fast to her Midwestern morals in Pleasant Company's efforts to do right by little girls. "Mothers were tired of the sexualization of little girls, tired of making children grow up too fast," says Rowland. "They yearned for a product that would both capture their 'child's interest and allow little girls to be little girls for a little longer." The toy industry got the message: In 1998, Mattel bought Pleasant Company for $700 million. Now retired, Rowland shared her story—and her mania for execution—with FSB. —JULIE SLOANE

I started Pleasant Company when I was 45 and I'd already had several careers. I'd been an elementary-school teacher, a TV news reporter, the author of reading textbooks, and the publisher of a small magazine. I had no formal business education.

In 1984 my husband invited me to join him at a convention at Colonial Williamsburg. Off I went, thinking I was going to have a nice little vacation. Instead it turned into one of the seminal experiences of my life. I loved sitting in the pew where George Washington went to church and standing where Patrick Henry orated. I loved the costumes, the homes, the accessories of everyday life—all of it completely engaged me. I remember sitting on a bench in the shade, reflecting on what a poor job schools do of teaching history, and how sad it was that more kids couldn't visit this fabulous classroom of living history. Was there some way I could bring history alive for them, the way Williamsburg had for me?

The following Christmas my two nieces were 8 and 10 years old, and I wanted to give them each a doll. To my horror, that was the Christmas that Cabbage Patch Kids hit the market. I thought they were ugly, and Barbie wasn't what I had in mind either. Here I was, in a generation of women at the forefront of redefining women's roles, and yet our daughters were playing with dolls that celebrated being a teen queen or a mommy. I knew I couldn't be the only woman in America who was unhappy with these Christmas choices.

My Williamsburg experience and my Christmas shopping experience collided, and the concept literally exploded in my brain. I wrote a postcard to my closest friend, which is still in the archives of Pleasant Company. It said, "What do you think of this idea? A series of books about 9-year-old girls growing up in different times in history, with a doll for each of the characters and historically accurate clothes and accessories with which girls could play out the stories?" In essence, I would create a miniature version of the Colonial Williamsburg experience and take it to American girls using the very playthings—books and dolls—that girls have always loved. I wouldn't invent a new toy but rather add meaning and relevance to the most timeless ones.

Once the idea had formed, I could think of nothing else. In one weekend I wrote out the concept in great detail. I defined the first three characters, the product line, the series of books, the matching girls' clothing, the retail-store concept, even the idea for a musical. My pen flew as I tried to capture the idea that was just given to me—whole. This was my business plan!

Unlike most entrepreneurs, I did not have to beat the bushes

> ## "ONCE THE IDEA HAD FORMED, I COULD THINK OF NOTHING ELSE. IN ONE WEEKEND I WROTE OUT THE CONCEPT IN INCREDIBLE DETAIL."
>
> —PLEASANT ROWLAND *Pleasant Company*

---

for startup funding. I had saved $1.2 million from textbook royalties, and American Girl seemed like a million-dollar idea. I put $200,000 aside in case all failed and plunged in. Though I had experience creating books, I hadn't a clue how to make dolls or the myriad clothes and accessories I envisioned for them. I didn't even have a model of a cute doll, so I sent a friend to Chicago to find one. By the end of the second day, she found one at Marshall Field's, down in the storeroom, covered with dust. Nobody had paid any attention to this doll because it had crossed eyes! The sales clerk had no idea where it had come from, but when we undressed the doll, sewn inside the underpants was a label that said "Gotz Puppenfabrik, Rodental, West Germany." A series of letters and phone calls later, I was in Germany picking out fabrics and ribbons and clothes for the American Girl dolls.

While the dolls were being made in Germany, we produced the books in our own office and found vendors in China to make the miniature accessories. Our goal was to be in the market for Christmas of 1986. I hired a marketing manager, who recommended that we do a couple of focus groups, just for "peace of mind"—a prudent suggestion that had never crossed my mind. I remember sitting behind the mirrored glass window while the focus group leader described the American Girl concept to a group of mothers. They thought it was the worst idea they'd ever heard. They absolutely panned it. I was devastated—and terrified. It had never really entered my head that this idea could fail! Then during the second half of the focus group, the leader brought out the doll with a sample book, her little bed, and her clothes and accessories. Before our eyes, the same group of women did a 180. Complete flip-over. They loved it. The experience crystallized a very important lesson for me: Success isn't in the concept. It's in the execution.

And that's what's so exhausting for an entrepreneur. If you have a strong vision—and mine was incredibly detailed—you can't let any piece of its execution go. Everything has to be a ten. I knew there was magic in the American Girl concept, but it was in the whole idea, not just part. I knew the books had to have stories so good that the reader would identify with and fall in love with the character. If she loved the character, she would want the doll. If she had the doll, she would want the clothes and accessories to play out the stories. If she played out the stories, she would want more books. So nothing could disappoint. The product had to be right, down to the tiniest detail.

And once we got the product right, the marketing had to have some magic in it. It was clear to me that American Girl was a thinking girl's product line, one that would not sell at Toys 'R' Us. It wasn't meant to blare from the shelves on its packaging or visual appeal alone. It had a more important message—one that had to be delivered in a softer voice. A 30-second commercial couldn't do the job—a strategy we couldn't afford anyway. How could I get this message across to girls and their mothers? Direct mail was the answer—an industry that was rising fast. Lands' End is up the road from Pleasant Company. Good friends and neighbors who worked there were most generous in teaching me the basics of the business—even though they thought my product line would never work and told me so!

The list-management company advising us on our mailing list also thought American Girl was going to be a huge failure. They told us to mail no more than 100,000 catalogs. I said, "No way." We had to take our shot that Christmas, and American Girl would either succeed or fail. So we mailed 500,000 catalogs and crossed our fingers.

And American Girl took off. Between Sept. 1 and Dec. 31, 1986, we sold $1.7 million worth of product. For all the money the company made subsequently, none of it was as fun or rewarding as that first million dollars. That first Christmas we cobbled together packing stations out of plywood and old doors. We were in a broken-down warehouse with one freight elevator. Workers wore mittens because there was no reliable heat. The week before Christmas we ran out of bedspreads for one of the doll beds. We closed the offices so that everyone could sew more bedspreads to fill the Christmas orders. We lived on adrenaline.

In the second year sales grew to $7.6 million, and we outgrew our funky little warehouse and moved to a new building in a cornfield on the outskirts of town. Then, just as we finished setting up our new operation in time for our third Christmas, I was diagnosed with breast cancer. I cut the ribbon on the new warehouse in the morning and went into the hospital that afternoon to have surgery. It was a large tumor, and I had a poor prognosis, but throughout chemotherapy and radiation I never missed a day of work, and work is probably what

PLEASANT ROWLAND, 01
Pleasant Company, *Middleton, Wis.*

Innovation: *First company to recognize girls ages 7 to 12 as an underserved market. Also created black and Hispanic dolls coveted by children of all races.*

How it changed the world:
Pleasant Company clearly identified the intellectual and consumer appetite of the "tween" demographic. Combining collectible dolls with a series of books made playing and learning fashionable.

Legacy: *The market uncovered by Pleasant Company didn't stay invisible for long. As Rowland's business grew, the 1990s also saw preteen girls becoming a core audience not only for books and dolls, but the music and entertainment industry. The Olsen twins, Britney Spears, and a bevy of boy bands all stand on the shoulders of tween girls, an annual market of $93 billion in the U.S.*

saved me. Pleasant Company was on such a roll. I loved what I was doing, and, after all, my mind 'didn't have cancer. I just got through.

In the next four years the American Girl brand grew to $77 million, fueled only by direct-mail catalogs and word of mouth. It was hot with young girls, an audience largely ignored before. To expand the brand, we created Bitty Baby dolls and books for younger girls, and for older girls we created modern girl dolls, *American Girl* magazine, and a line of advice books about friendships and social interactions. Sales grew in the next five years to almost $ 300 million in about $ 50 million increments each year.

> "I HAD NEVER FELT I OWNED AMERICAN GIRL. I HAD BEEN ITS STEWARD, AND I HAD GIVEN IT MY BEST. IT WAS TIME TO TAKE CARE OF IT."

The last important piece of the original business plan came into being with the building of American Girl Place in Chicago and the launch of a musical there, *The American Girls Revue*. This would be the American Girl mecca, an extremely special environment with a store, a theater, a museum, and a restaurant. American Girl Place opened for Christmas 1998, grossing $40 million a year from the day it opened.

Finally my vision was complete, my original business plan had been executed, and I was tired. It was time to sell the company. I sold American Girl to Mattel for $700 million. Why Mattel? I felt a genuine connection to [then CEO] Jill Barad, the woman who built Barbie. The ironies did not escape me, and many were critical of my decision, but I saw in Jill a blend of passion, perfectionism, and perseverance with real business savvy. During the same 13-year period that I built American Girl from zero to $300 million, Jill built Barbie from $200 million to $2 billion. An amazing feat.

I'll never forget the day I signed the papers to complete the sale. The documents were just sitting in my in basket as innocently as any memo. I waited until the end of the day, signed them, and headed home. As I walked out the door, I stopped and looked around at all I had built, expecting to be overwhelmed by sadness or loss. But no emotion came. I drove home thinking, What's wrong? Why don't I feel anything? It was then I realized that I had never felt I "owned" American Girl. I had been its steward, and I had given it my very best during the prime of my career. It was time for someone else to take care of it. American Girl was a wonderful chapter in my life that is now closed. And on we go.

VISIONARY CHUCK WILLIAMS ON WILLIAMS-SONOMA

If not for Chuck Williams, your salads would be bereft of that splash of balsamic vinegar, your pasta might lack that oomph given by a shot of garlic from a garlic press, and holiday cookies might take until February to get to the oven without a timesaving KitchenAid standing mixer. A founding father of the American "foodie" movement, Williams sold the country on those and many other condiments and kitchen tools, which he first stocked at Williams-Sonoma, the gourmet specialty shop he created from a defunct hardware store in 1956. Since then, his little shop and catalog have morphed into a retailing and mail-order giant that's moved beyond the kitchen and now includes Pottery Barn, Hold Everything, Chambers, and West Elm, a new contemporary home-furnishings catalog. In 2005 the company posted $3.5 billion in revenue and operates over 500 stores. Here's how Williams transformed a rural Northern California hardware store into a gourmet haven, permanently altering the American kitchen and the national palate. —ARLYN TOBIAS GAJILAN

My first memories of being in the kitchen were with my grandmother, who had a restaurant in Lima, Ohio, when she was younger. When she'd make divinity fudge or a lemon meringue pie, she would have me beat the egg whites for her. This was before electric mixers, so I had to use a big oval platter and a fork. It took forever, but I didn't mind. Being in the kitchen with her made me happy.

Happiness was in short supply during the Depression. My father's auto-repair business went to pot and finally closed. Not finding work, he decided that we should move to California. Being a teenager, I found a job picking fruit for pennies. My father still couldn't find work and felt he was a burden on us, and he finally just left me, my mother, and my sister to fend for ourselves. I saw him only once after that. Consequently I grew up pretty fast. My mother decided that we should move to the desert—near Palm Springs—where I got a job on a date ranch.

Those weren't easy times, but I did begin to experience the things that influenced me years later when I opened Williams-Sonoma. I moved in with the family who owned the date ranch and began working in their roadside shop, both helping customers and packing dates and grapefruit, after my sister, Marie, suddenly died at age 19 and my mother moved back to Florida. I became expert at dealing with discriminating customers, which were mostly what we had back then. People who could afford to be tourists during the Depression had money, and they were very clear on how they spent it.

Knowing how to treat customers and having a few carpentry

"BACK THEN, THE DEPARTMENT STORES PILED POTS AND PANS ON TABLES IN HEAPS. I DIDN'T DO THAT,"

—CHUCK WILLIAMS, *founder of Williams-Sonoma.*

---

skills helped me land other retail jobs. I worked at Bullock's department store in Los Angeles, where I was in the window-dressing department. From there I got a job at I. Magnin in Hollywood. This was during the golden age of personal shopping when women expected to be waited on hand and foot. Many wouldn't even come into the store; they'd call a favorite salesperson to send them dresses, shoes, hats, and gloves on approval.

Before World War II, I tried to enlist in the Air Force, but examining doctors said I had a thyroid condition and wouldn't sign me up. Anxious to do something for the war effort, I worked on the assembly lines for Lockheed Aircraft and later volunteered to be part of its traveling maintenance crew. We were stationed in East Africa and India. I was pretty busy, but I managed to develop a taste for investigating the countryside in my free time. I visited small towns and villages to sample the local foods, coffees, and some of the strongest homemade alcohol I've ever had.

After the war I returned to Los Angeles. I hooked up with one of my overseas buddies and visited Sonoma to play golf, and I just fell in love with the place. I soon moved there, bought a small piece of property, and built a house for myself. I immediately got my contractor's license, and by 1953, I had built or renovated quite a few houses for other people and was living pretty comfortably in Sonoma as a contractor.

CHUCK WILLIAMS, 88
Startup year: 1956

First Venture:
Williams opened a cooking store in a summer resort town called Sonoma at age 41. Heard of it?

Inspiration:
The Great Depression. "After living through it, I never wanted to be poor again."

Darkest Hour:
Williams's partner died in 1978. With the company heavily in debt, Williams wanted out and sold the business.

Turning Point:
The company's 1983 IPO let it expand beyond the kitchen. "The money we raised helped buy Pottery Barn, Hold Everything, and Chambers."

I got the idea for Williams-Sonoma in 1953 after two friends and I decided to splurge and take a trip to Europe. Knowing how to cook and being interested in eating, I was fascinated with Paris. I spent about two weeks there, sampling small restaurants and seeing all the wonderful cooking equipment that was available to the French home cook. There were so many things we didn't have in this country, such as heavy sauté pans, huge stockpots, fish poachers, and an endless array of bakeware. There was no difference between what home cooks and restaurants used. But in this country, what home cooks could buy were relatively inexpensive pots and pans, made out of thin aluminum or tin.

I began thinking that Sonoma was a good place to start a business selling what I'd found in France. Sonoma was just a country town back then, but lots of people from San Francisco had summer homes there. And a small group of us were fans of French cooking and had a kind of regular rotating dinner party. So I bought a building downtown with a hardware store. My intention was to transform the place into a series of shops, including one of my own.

The first Williams-Sonoma opened just before Christmas 1956. As with my house construction, I remodeled everything myself. I covered the floor in a checkerboard of black and white tile and painted the walls a brilliant shade of yellow I'd seen in pictures of Russian houses. Back then most people bought pots and pans in department and hardware stores, which usually piled them on tables in heaps. I didn't do that. Not many people in this country had seen some of the things we were selling, so I thought you should see each pan in the best possible way. I put them up on a shelf in size order, with all the handles facing the same way, ensuring that anyone walking in would see the display at its best angle. If somebody wanted to buy something, he had to ask me to get it for him, thus creating conversation. As in the upscale stores I had worked in, I tried to build the place so that it demanded that customers be served. That approach made us interact and let me talk up French cooking.

Almost as soon as I opened, friends and customers pressed me to move the shop to San Francisco. In early 1958, I listened. Several told me location would be key, and I found a storefront just off Union Square on an upscale shopping block. That location didn't come cheap. I signed what was then a rather expensive ten-year lease, at $400 a month or 10 percent of gross sales, whichever was bigger. That first year the shop grossed $35,000. Sales increased yearly, so my landlord realized a pretty nice bargain.

I may not have understood real estate contracts, but I knew how to take advantage of the rising interest in fine food. By 1961 a few cookbooks that were a step above the Fannie Farmer variety started showing up. Among them was Julia Child's Mastering the Art of French Cooking, which was followed by her TV show the next year. She really encouraged people to cook, and as her show began to find an audience, we found more customers. One night she showed how to make a soufflé, and the next day people came in asking about soufflé dishes. Around this time, James Beard, now renowned as the dean of American cooking, came in, and we became good friends. He and other notable food writers of the day helped spread the word.

Other customers helped too. Jackie Mallorca, a copywriter for a local advertising agency and a store regular, suggested that a mail-order catalog would help build business beyond the Bay Area. I don't like taking gambles, so I sat on it for awhile. I was lucky enough to ask the advice of Edward Marcus, who was also a customer and happened to run the Neiman Marcus catalog. He thought the timing made sense, and Jackie and I created the first catalog in 1971.

When I say catalog, I'm being a bit generous. That first one was simple—black and white—and fit into business-sized envelopes. Our mailing list had only about 5,000 names, but we printed 10,000 copies so we had extra to give away in the shop. Local purchases were sent free via UPS. Since credit cards hadn't yet appeared, we opened charge accounts for almost anyone. If you needed to return something, you could send it back without hassle. That kind of customer service kept people shopping.

To keep the store and catalog stocked with new items, I took trips to France every January. Garlic presses, lemon zesters, ice-cream makers, and food processors are the kinds of things people take for granted now. But before they found a place in American kitchens, Williams-Sonoma sold them. Not everyone was convinced they'd sell widely, not even the manufacturers. The KitchenAid stand mixer, for example, could be bought only at restaurant-supply stores or through Avon-like parties. I approached the manufacturer, Hobart, and soon had them to sell. It was expensive compared with other mixers, but it became a must-have and a top seller for both us and Hobart.

Right from the beginning I filled the store with what I wanted to see in my kitchen, and always attracted customers that liked what I like. That was true for both cooking equipment and food. I was in Milan visiting one of my favorite stores and saw a pretty, frosted hexagonal bottle filled with something that looked like hair tonic to me. Not being able to read Italian, I was unsure of what it was, but I bought it anyway. The store's owner later explained that it was a condiment that farmers traditionally made for themselves or sold at roadside stands. The tradition was dying out as farmers' kids began moving to the city. What I'd bought and later distributed through Williams-Sonoma turned out to be balsamic vinegar. That was a great success story for us.

Those kinds of discoveries earned us a bit of a cult following. By 1972 the store was doing pretty well, the mail-order business kept growing, and I was having trouble keeping up. For 17 years we'd stayed a one-store business. Like lots of entrepreneurs, I did everything myself, from sweeping the sidewalk to balancing the books. But when it came to the business end of things, I was smart enough to know I didn't know enough to expand.

I turned to Edward Marcus again. He advised incorporating, and he and a couple of his friends bought about 50 percent of the company. Eddie contributed advice while I continued to search for new and different things. In 1973 we opened a second store, in Beverly Hills on Rodeo Drive. That was followed up with stores in Palo Alto and Costa Mesa. Meanwhile, the catalog had been redesigned, and the mail-order business had grown so much by 1977 that we had to open a small distribution center. Things seemed as if they were going pretty well.

Finally Eddie realized we needed an overall manager and hired a friend of his. A few months later Eddie died. It was a personal blow but also a financial one. Through a couple of unfortunate decisions by the new management, the company was quickly in debt. The company had about $4 million in sales, but we posted a net loss of $173,000. I'm not a financier, but I knew we were in trouble and I'd have to sell. By that point, I just wanted the easiest way out. My lawyer found a buyer—Howard Lester, who used to work at IBM. He bought the company on the condition that I stay on to select the merchandise and run the catalog. Lester's the one who got things turned around.

I know you're supposed to feel happy when the company you founded goes public, but I wasn't when we went public in 1983. It's not your company anymore. You can be part of it, but it's not yours. Still, the company really grew after that. Slowly Lester expanded the business by buying the Gardener's

---

"I KNOW THAT YOU'RE SUPPOSED TO FEEL
HAPPY WHEN YOU GO PUBLIC, BUT I WASN'T.
IT'S NOT YOUR COMPANY ANYMORE."

Eden catalog, then later the Pottery Barn stores. By 1986, Williams-Sonoma had its first $100 million year. I stayed focused on merchandise but also began writing and editing cookbooks. In 1991 the first books of the Williams-Sonoma Kitchen Library Series were published. Since then, I've written several more cookbooks and edited over 150. In the decade since, over 17 million Williams-Sonoma books have been sold.

I don't think of us as a huge company, though, but as one store. That's my approach when I select merchandise, which I still do. One of my more recent finds was the Dualit toaster. I spotted it at a classic design shop in Paris and just thought it was beautiful and something that would look good even 100 years from now. The least expensive model sells for $199, but it's been a phenomenon. We sold more than 25,000 last year. I still recommend what appeals to me and what I think represents good design. I think people will always respond to that.

VISIONARY EARL GRAVES ON BLACK ENTERPRISE

For many black kids growing up in the Brooklyn neighborhood of Bedford-Stuyvesant, the color of money has often seemed very white. That didn't sit well with Earl G. Graves, who was raised in that tough neighborhood during the '40s and '50s. He came of age during the civil rights era and has spent most of his professional life trying through charm, editorializing, and cajolery to bring about a shift in America's balance of wealth and power that would help any person of color succeed. His bully pulpit: Black Enterprise magazine. Launched in 1970, it was the first publication ever devoted to African-American entrepreneurs and corporate executives. With a $175,000 Small Business Administration startup loan, Graves created a media empire that in 2003 generated $55 million in revenues.

Building on his flagship magazine's reputation, Graves and his three sons have also been diversifying their interests. The family con-

cern now includes a personal-finance and business-book publishing house, an executive-conferences division, and a $90 million private-equity fund that invests exclusively in minority-owned or -managed businesses. Graves says that the fund, launched in 1997, has done so well that he's creating another. Not bad for a kid from Bed-Stuy. From his offices on Fifth Avenue, Graves, 72, recounts how he started out in Brooklyn, found his way working alongside Bobby Kennedy, and created a magazine as dedicated to social justice as it is to business.

—ARLYN TOBIAS GAJILAN

Until I was 32, my life revolved around Brooklyn and my church. I mostly sold neighborhood real estate and dabbled in local politics. What I did was very parochial. That changed during the 1960s. Back then you would have had to be blind not to see the world changing around you. It was impossible for me to be apolitical, so in 1964 I walked into the local Democratic headquarters near election time. The sight of a well-dressed black man volunteering to sign up must have put off someone, because I got the cold shoulder. I did what was typical for me: I wrote a letter to the chairman of the Democratic National Committee. He told me to report to the New York State Democratic campaign headquarters,

---

EARL G. GRAVES, 72
CHAIRMAN
and CEO
Startup year: 1969

First Venture:
"I was not in a community where you could cut grass," says Graves. At age 7 he sold Christmas cards door to door. Even then, he "romanced the sale" by placing cards he thought a customer might like best at the top of the box.

Inspiration:
His father, a garment-district salesman. "He was the best at it. If a winter coat was $10 and a woman tried to get him down to $7, he would offer to sell her two coats at $9 each."

Darkest Hour:
As an aide to R.F.K., watching the life spill out of him and onto the kitchen floor of the Ambassador Hotel.

Turning Point:
Taking a Ford fellowship in 1968 to study black entrepreneurship, rather than a steady job at IBM.

and I did. I was put to work as a volunteer on the Lyndon Johnson-Hubert Humphrey ticket, which encompassed Robert Kennedy's bid for the U.S. Senate. At Christmastime in 1964, Kennedy's campaign decided to host children's holiday parties in each of New York City's five boroughs. I offered to plan the one in Brooklyn. Each of the other parties was plagued by problems. At one, someone even stole all the kids' gifts.

Not on my turf, though. When Bobby stepped out of his car in front of the National Guard's 13th Regiment Armory in Brooklyn, he was greeted by comedian Soupy Sales and a local drum-and-bugle corps playing "Jingle Bells." Once inside, Kennedy was almost blasted backward by a ringing "Hallelujah Chorus" from a full gospel choir. Kennedy turned to a smiling young man at his side, looked him in the eye, and said, "This is really very good. Tell me your name again." I said, "Graves. Earl G. Graves."

Soon after, I joined Kennedy's staff as an administrative assistant. I was now working for an icon from a family of icons. Kennedy's world was filled with a steady stream of power brokers, elite athletes, and other celebrities. His world of power and privilege became accessible to me as one of his aides. In turn, I shared my world: Brooklyn and the voters that other politicians had often ignored. When he announced his presidential candidacy in 1968, we were all optimistic that his dedication to civil rights and social justice would change the country.

June 5, 1968, was a turning point for a lot of people, including myself. That night Bobby Kennedy was shot. I saw him lying on the kitchen floor of the Ambassador Hotel in Los Angeles, and blood was running out the back of his head. Tragedy was written all over that moment. It was a sad time for the country and an uncertain time for me personally. Who anticipates their employer being assassinated? I didn't have a plan B for that eventuality, but I still had to feed my wife and three young sons.

Fortunately, having been a Kennedy staffer marked me as

highly employable. I was offered both a job with IBM and a Ford Foundation fellowship. Those were IBM's halcyon days, and a job there would have been a steady meal ticket. But to me it sounded like fixed income. I didn't want any limitations on what I thought I could earn. I wanted to be my own boss. So I accepted the Ford fellowship, essentially a work-study grant. Contemp-lating a career as a consultant to black businesspeople, I studied entrepreneurship and economic development in Barbados, where my grandparents were from. When I came back, I set out to advise business on tapping an emerging black market.

There are probably some entrepreneurs who will tell you they were lying in bed at 6 a.m. and heard the voice of God telling them to start a business. I didn't get any such call. I had thought about starting a newsletter to help with my consulting. But a few people, like Howard Samuels, a friend from my Kennedy days and then head of the Small Business Administration, suggested I should think bigger and start a magazine instead.

By the late '60s there were roughly 100,000 black businesses in the country, and most were mom-and-pop operations. But Samuels knew—and I agreed—that the number would grow. The Civil Rights Act of 1964 cleared the way for policies designed to level the playing field for minority-owned businesses. In 1968 the SBA launched a program to help minority-owned firms compete for government contracts. In 1969, President Nixon signed Executive Order 11458, which directed the Secretary of Commerce to coordinate the federal government's efforts to promote minority enterprise, in effect creating the Minority Business Development Agency.

That's the environment Black Enterprise magazine was created in. With the support of my wife, I took out a $175,000 SBA-backed loan in 1969. We were about to become the only publication devoted to black entrepreneurs and rising corporate executives. We were determined to put the words "black" and "capitalism" in the same sentence. Interestingly, it was also the year the first man walked on the moon, proving nothing was impossible. By 1970 our team published our inaugural issue with the following mission statement: "Lacking capital, managerial and technical knowledge, and crippled by prejudice, the minority businessman has been effectively kept out of the American marketplace. We want to help change this."

That wasn't easy to do early on. Time and again, I had to educate white advertisers about the black consumer. I ran around trying to convince people that black people smoke, drive cars, stay in hotels, and have credit cards. That wasn't easy. Then again, "easy" has never been a part of black people's vocabulary. Even before our first issue, I developed a media kit. Some of the copy is anathema to me now, because in many ways we pandered to a white audience. Some of the images and text we used hinted that advertising with us would be doing the right thing. While it was important to reference the recent civil rights movement, I'd do things differently today and focus more on why it's simply smart business to advertise with us.

Still, our early strategy worked. Our first long-term advertiser wrote a check for a full year of ads before the magazine hit newsstands. That was Carter Products, maker of Carter's Little Liver Pills. They were supposed to be so effective that even after you died, your liver would still be flapping around and you'd have to beat it to death with a stick. In that first year we had $900,000 in ad revenues, and the magazine was profitable by its tenth issue.

The year we first published, there were only three black people among the 3,000 serving as directors on boards of Fortune 500 companies. But I was convinced more would follow. At the time we were one of the few media outlets to cover African-Americans in a way that respected their aspirations in the workplace, encouraged them to start businesses, and advised them to invest their hard-earned dollars. While major business publications like Business Week, Fortune, and The Wall Street Journal largely ignored the challenges and triumphs of black professionals, we were quick to cover them in full. In 1973 we started the BE-100, a ranking of the top 100 black-owned businesses in the country. And it was Black Enterprise that first wrote about the late dealmaker Reginald Lewis, whose TLC Beatrice was the first black-owned billion-dollar Fortune 500 company. It was us that foretold the rise of Avis's Barry Rand, Maytag's Lloyd Ward, Symantec's John Thompson, and American Express's Ken Chenault to the CEO's chair of their respective companies.

After 33 years of publishing, we are still growing. With the help of my three sons—Earl Jr. "Butch," Johnny, and Michael—who all work in the business, we're building on the firm foundation created by the magazine, which now has 375,000 sub-

> "WE PUT 'BLACK' AND 'CAPITALISM'
> IN THE SAME SENTENCE. IT WAS THE
> YEAR MAN WALKED ON THE MOON.
> NOTHING WAS IMPOSSIBLE."

scribers. Our credibility with readers and corporate America has helped us create a popular series of executive conferences, including the Black Enterprise/Microsoft Entrepreneurs Conference, the nation's largest gathering of African-American entrepreneurs. In collaboration with John Wiley & Sons, we've also expanded into personal-finance and business-book publishing. All our titles are by and about African-Americans. And with the success of our business and additional financing from Citigroup, I created the Black Enterprise/Greenwich Street Corporate Growth fund, a $90 million private-equity fund that invests in minority-owned or -managed companies. That fund has maxed out, and we're looking at starting another one along similar lines. We're also getting ready for a TV joint venture.

All those things are happening because of my sons. But Butch still has to knock on doors and educate advertisers, just as I did three decades ago. Our income as a community is now

"I BUILT A MAGAZINE TO TEACH THE BLACK ENTREPRENEUR HOW TO TAP INTO THE BILLIONS OF DOLLARS WE GENERATE. THAT'S BLACK POWER,"

in excess of $600 billion, placing us as the ninth- or tenth-largest nation in the world in terms of income. Racism is a terrible thing, and it's alive and well. But my sons are making progress convincing companies that black consumers can afford their products. Because of them, our company's best days are still in front of it."

VISIONARY LES WEXNER ON LIMITED BRANDS

When Leslie Wexner was in college, he really wanted to become an architect. His father, however, didn't think that was a good idea. As it turns out, sometimes fathers do know best. Following his dad's advice—and his footsteps—Wexner opened a women's clothing store called the Limited in Columbus, Ohio, in 1963. Unlike his father, whose shop went bankrupt, Wexner aggressively grew his own into an empire that today includes such brands as Victoria's Secret, Bath & Body Works, Express, Limited Stores, Henri Bendel, and more. Wexner—who as a kid hated the very idea of retail—now oversees more than 3,800 locations. Revenues in 2005 were $9.7 billion, and Limited Brands was voted Most Admired Specialty Retailer in Fortune's 2002 rankings.

Wexner's stores pretty much ruled the suburban shopping malls until the 1990s, when the company was criticized for losing both direction and profits. In an effort to streamline the business, Wexner made major changes—selling off faltering brands like Lane Bryant and

Lerner New York and buying back the previously spun-off Intimate Brands (made up of Victoria's Secret and Bath & Body Works). "As an entrepreneur," says Wexner, who's been self-employed since age 9, "you work out solutions." From Limited Brands' corporate headquarters, which he designed (he says he still wishes he'd become an architect), Wexner talks about the family of brands he created. — CARLYE ADLER

Growing up, I knew you were supposed to have a profession—and something better than being a shopkeeper, which is what my parents were. I didn't want to go into the retail business. I hated it. My father had been a store manager at a small chain of specialty stores, and when I was 15, he took his life savings and invested it in his own women's clothing store. My parents named it Leslie's, after me. They worked 80-hour weeks to scratch out a living, but they never made $10,000 a year.

When you grow up in a family like that, if you want another pair of jeans or a bike or toys, you have to work for it. An allowance was out of the question, so I always had jobs. My first one was cutting grass and shoveling snow when I was 9 years old. When it snowed, I was happy because I could work—not because I could go sledding. If it rained in the summer, that was good because the grass would grow and I could cut more lawns. It meant money. As I look back it seems

LESLIE WEXNER, 69
CEO
Startup year: 1963

First Venture:
Among other kid stuff, babysitting: "In hindsight, I understood leverage. Instead of making 25 cents an hour with one kid, I could take ten kids to the park for two hours for the same rate."

Inspiration:
His father, who ran a women's clothing store. "He was very wise and had good judgment about people and ideas."

Darkest Hour:
"Before I could change my business model in the early '90s, I needed to change from sole inventor to the leader, the teacher, the coach. The darkest time, but also enlightening."

Turning Point:
His first year, 1963. "We did $160,000 in sales-$60,000 more than my best estimate and more than my dad ever made in a year."

kind of Dickensian, but it didn't feel that way to me at the time.

After college I decided to go to law school. I still wasn't interested in retail, but I'd take study breaks from some boring case and, just for amusement, draw designs for stores and storefronts. Some people made erotic drawings or wrote their girlfriend's name—I did stores.

Before long, I dropped out of law school; I hated it because it wasn't creative enough. My dad asked me to hang around the store for a few months to learn how to take the money to the bank and close each night so that he and my mom could take a vacation. They hadn't taken one in ten years. I learned how to run the store and take the money to the bank, and they spent a week in Miami. While they were gone, I started some simple accounting to see what categories and goods made the most money. It was just curiosity, but I figured out pretty quickly that my dad made money selling skirts, sweaters, shirts, and blouses—typical sportswear separates—and he lost his ass selling dresses and coats. When my father came back, I asked him where he made money. He said dresses and coats.

Then we got into a typical father-son wrangle: "You're not going to tell me how to run the business," he said. "I worked my whole life. Get a job. You don't know anything about retailing." He was right, I didn't. But I did know a little about accounting, and I decided to prove that my theory was right and that he had it wrong.

When I first thought about the store I wanted to create, I called it Leslie's Limited. It was to be my limited store—meaning it would have a limited assortment, and I would sell only women's sportswear separates. Besides what I learned from my parents' store, the idea of specialization was very popular at the time. My friends were going to be doctors, but they were going to be specialists, not general practitioners. Lawyers were going to become tax lawyers. I began thinking about the business being a specialist—it was the only way I thought I could compete against the department stores that were dominant at the time.

I had a spinster aunt who loaned me $5,000 to get started, and on top of that a bank loaned me $5,000. I was on my way. I figured out a lease, designed the store, and built it myself. But in the seven months before it opened, I'd wake up in the middle of the night screaming. I had a recurring dream that I was opening a store, and I can remember going to the door, unlocking it, and seeing people standing with their noses pressed to the door—but no one walked in. It was a terrible nightmare. About two weeks before the store opened, I called my family doctor and told him my stomach hurt after I ate. The doctor said, "You're too young for an ulcer." (I was 26 years old.) Then they took an X-ray of my stomach, and I had an ulcer.

The first store opened in Columbus on Aug. 10, 1963. First-day sales were negligible, $473, but that was still amazing to me. By January, after the fall and the holiday season, I was pretty sure I'd had a good idea. First-year sales totaled $160,000—I did more business and made more money than my dad ever made in a year. And in the second year it tripled.

I opened the second store in August 1964. (I'd leased the second store before the first one opened, so if it had failed, I would've been in a hell of a mess.) When my dad found out that I was going to open a second store, he quit talking to me for almost a year. He thought I was crazy. I respected my dad's judgment, but he was always cautious. He came to this country from Russia when he was a teenager. He was immensely proud and very conservative. When I had two stores, he said, "You're winning, take it to the bank." At four stores, he said, "You're winning, take it to the bank." When we had six stores, I decided I wanted to become a public company, and he thought I was totally insane. Everybody did. They said, "Your friends and acquaintances will buy stock, and then everybody will wallpaper their johns with it." In 1969 we went public with an intrastate offering, so the only people who could buy stock were residents of Ohio. We were too small for an interstate offering, too small for the SEC. It's unheard-of today.

Over the 20 year period that Jack Welch ran GE, the

Limited was one of the few companies to increase its share price faster than GE. People retired from very simple jobs here—distribution-center workers, maintenance associates—who made millions of dollars.

We had stores in San Francisco, and that's where I found an interesting little lingerie store called Victoria's Secret. It was a small store, and it was Victorian—not English Victorian but brothel Victorian, with red-velvet sofas. There wasn't erotic lingerie, but there was very sexy lingerie, and I hadn't seen anything like it in all my travels.

Victoria's Secret was started by a fellow named Roy Raymond, who created the business as an MBA project while at Stanford. I was curious to learn more, but he was very guarded. When I met him, it was as if he met the devil. We were this big company with dozens and dozens of stores. He had three stores. Nothing happened from the meeting, but six months later he called me and said he was going to be put into bankruptcy that week. He'd rather sell the company to me than go bankrupt.

I got on a plane to San Francisco that day, and within 24 hours we negotiated the purchase. The idea was to buy the business and park it. I didn't know anything about the lingerie business, but then I began thinking—as a bachelor. (I got married later in life.) Most of the women I knew wore underwear, and most of them would rather wear lingerie. I thought maybe we could re-conceptualize it into a business—instead of selling underwear, we could market and position it as lingerie. I thought if we could develop price points and products that had a broader customer base, it could be something big. It's our most profitable business today, but it didn't take off like a rocket. We just got better and better at it, and understood it more and more.

Pretty soon Abercrombie & Fitch and Lerner New York came along. We also acquired an Henri Bendel store in New York, and opened Limited Too, fashion for girls, and opened our first men's store, Structure (now called Express Men). Acquiring businesses pretty much carried us through the 1980s. By the early '90s we were a multi-division company. We had a lot of businesses. But I started to ask myself, How do you control these businesses? How do you run them? I came to the conclusion that we were more like a venture-capital company than a multi-division company. We didn't have the systems, processes, organization, or leadership for any kind of central organization. Every day I came to work and felt as though it was a zoo. All the cages were open, and the animals were running around. It all culminated one day when I met Jack Welch of GE. He told me the way he thinks about managing the top talent in the business. I was sure that I knew and influenced the top people, but then I found out we didn't even know who the top people were. We didn't know how many officers there were in the different businesses. And we certainly didn't have the discipline to oversee it all; I learned that somebody had made their administrative assistant a vice president.

It was as if one day the emperor realized he had no clothes. We didn't have any real organization. We spent the next year reading and understanding what multi-division companies are like at their center. I decided that we needed to imagine our-

---

"WE DIDN'T HAVE ANY CENTRAL ORGANIZATION. I CAME TO WORK AND IT FELT LIKE A ZOO WITH ALL THE CAGES OPEN."

—LES WEXNER, *founder of Limited Brands*

---

selves as a very complex organism, or an animal with a central nervous system. We needed a center to help us grow it into the future and develop the appropriate processes and procedures that a large multi-division company should have. It was tough because everyone kind of liked it the way it was—the lack of discipline and the ability to make very decentralized decisions— because everyone saw himself or herself as an entrepreneur.

A woman at the Limited once asked me, "Why do you work?" She said, "You made a lot of money as a young man, so why are you still working?" I had never thought about it before. Forced to consider it, I told her, "You know why? Because I think that if you stop to smell the roses, you'll get hit by a truck." Sometimes I wish I lived more in the day, but I'm happier thinking about tomorrow or the day after. The way I see it, there's always a new or next thing."

PUTTING A STOP TO MOM AND POP

By Tom Stemberg

Like all great business ideas, Tom Stemberg's makes you wonder why nobody had ever thought of it before. A supermarket for office supplies—why, smack my forehead! But great ideas are products of their times. Staples was conceived in the mid-1980s, on the verge of the longest-running economic boom in U.S. history. A boom, moreover, driven not by corporate America, which has known all along where to buy cheap pencils, but by entrepreneurial America, which took to the Staples concept—huge selection, deep discounts, and long hours—like oxygen molecules rushing to fill a vacuum.

If Stemberg, now 57, had a rare feel for the new market he was serving, it's because he was part of it himself. After graduating from Harvard Business School, he spent 12 years climbing the corporate ladder, first at Jewel's Star Market, then at First National Supermarkets. When First National sold Stemberg's Edwards-Finast division from under him in 1985, he was out of a job and eager to start something on his own. "I felt I was ready to run a business," Stemberg says now. "I didn't like the politics of big companies."

Starting with a single store in Brighton, Mass., Stemberg built what today is a $16 billion company with more than 1,500 retail outlets, spawned three major copycat competitors, and forever changed the *way we look at list prices for paper clips. Early in 2002 he relinquished the CEO title to Ronald Sargent. Still chairman, Stemberg spends more time now on his small portfolio of startups. His story of how Staples began dispels what he calls "the single greatest myth about entrepreneurs—the swashbuckling, seat-of-the-pants image." Says Stemberg: "I've spent a lot of time talking to Michael Dell and Fred Smith [Federal Express]. Most great entrepreneurs are extremely analytical. Once they finally pull the trigger, no question, they run like hell. But not before they calculate the downsides and the risks very, very carefully." —DAVID WHITFORD*

For me there was no one eureka moment with Staples—it was a confluence of moments. I had just left my job at First National Supermarkets, and I was being recruited by the new industry of the mid-'80s, the wholesale clubs. Sam's had just started up—Price Club, Costco, Makro. So I go down to Langhorne, Pa., for an interview with Makro. Why? Because the Harvard basketball team had never beaten Princeton and Penn on the road in the same weekend, ever, and I thought they had a shot to do it that year (in fact, they ultimately did). Anyway, Langhorne is halfway between Princeton and Penn. I wanted to see those games and figured this was a free way of getting down there.

So I'm being interviewed by the CEO of Makro. And I said, "You know, this is not going to work in the U.S. Maybe if it just became a superstore, though, like a Toys 'R' Us for office supplies." Those were the words I used. At that point it registered as an idea I should think about. So I started thinking about it. There was a lawyer I knew in Hartford, which is where I lived then. If ever there was a cheap bastard in this world, he was a cheap bastard. And I said, "Gee, how much do you spend on office supplies?" He said, "Oh, I don't know, I guess about a couple of hundred bucks a person, 40 people in the office—I bet you we spend a grand." I said, "Do me a favor, will you? You've got good records. Go through your records and tell me exactly how much you spend." He calls me up the next day:

"Son of a bitch! I spend $ 1,000 apiece! But I'm getting a discount. I'm paying 10 percent off list." I said, "Toys 'R' Us is paying 60 percent off list." He says, "Are you kidding me? You mean I could save, like, half? I could save like 12 grand?" In his mind this is the payment on his new Jaguar.

Now I'm thinking, You know, this has some real potential. Big market. People want to save money. They don't realize they're getting hosed. I began doing some work. It was a Friday, Fourth of July weekend. Have you ever been to Hartford? Hartford is a miserable place. On the weekends everybody leaves. They go to New York. They go to Boston. They go to the seashore. They go to the mountains. There's nobody there. But I'm working my butt off. And the ribbon on my ImageWriter printer from my Apple IIC computer goes. And I need a new ribbon. So the first thing I do, I drive down to the local office-supply store in downtown West Hartford, called Plimptons, and it's closed. I go around the corner into Business Land, same thing. I drive up to BJ's Wholesale Club, and it had good prices on the printer ribbons it carried, but mine was not one of them. I said, "Oh, I'm fucked." As an entrepreneur, not only do you get ripped off when you can actually buy this stuff, but many times you can't buy it at all!

> "THE MYTH ABOUT ENTREPRENEURS IS THAT THEY'RE THESE SWASHBUCKLING, SEAT-OF-THE PANTSTYPES WHO JUST PLUNGE IN."
>
> —TOM STEMBERG, *founder of Staples*

Then I also had a mentor, a guy named Walter Salmon, the retail guru who teaches at Harvard Business School. I had lunch with Walter one day during the time I was thinking about all this stuff. I told him about a supermarket deal I was looking at. And he sort of leaned back, you know: "Tom, do you in your heart of hearts believe you can out-execute Shaws and Stop & Shop [two big New England chains]?" And I said,

"Walter, I think we can be different. I wouldn't say we could out-execute them. They're both very good." He said, "Well, as an alternative, have you thought about applying your distribution skills to a category that is both growing faster and less well served by modern distribution channels?"Those were his exact words. And I said, "Well, as a matter of fact, I have: office products." And he said, "Gee, this is a really big idea."

At one point I spent $20,000 and hired a woman who had been Walt Salmon's teaching assistant and had her validate the market for us. I'll never forget the night I went to her house and we went through the slide deck. I always want to jump ahead. And she puts her hand on my hand and says, "Wait, we'll walk through it." She's teasing us! Finally she said it was a $45 billion market growing at 15 percent a year. And it turns out she was lying. That was actually at the manufacturer level. It was actually more than $100 billion at that point already, if you looked at retail. She confirmed that the pricing umbrellas were as big as we thought they were, and that small business-es were being raped the way we had said they were. I was pret-ty excited during the long drive home.

Now, Wharton, at the University of Pennsylvania, had done a study of the office-products industry. It was wonderful. Essentially they first asked dealers, "What does the customer want?" Ninety percent of the dealers said, "Better service" and 10 percent said, "Other." Then they asked the customers, and 90 percent of the customers said what they really wanted were lower prices. Ha! The dealers were totally out of touch. They were making 40 percent to 50 percent, the wholesalers were making 30 percent, and the manufacturers were making huge margins. Everybody's rich, fat, and happy, and they're all going, "What's wrong with this?"

Until a guy like me came along, the answer was nothing. The manufacturers were under tremendous pressure from the dealers. You know, "If you sell to Staples, we'll shut you off." The worst was the Harvard Coop. The Harvard Coop told McKesson, the big wholesaler, that if it sold to Staples, the

Coop was going to shut them off. We actually went after the Harvard Coop. We did price-comparison ads with the Coop: "Why would somebody as smart as the Harvard student pay $3.68 for 79-cent-a-dozen pens?"

We were lucky, too, in that we had some great industry ties. William Blair, a venture firm in Chicago, was an investor in our company. They brought a bunch of companies public—including United Stationers, which today is still a big wholesaler. They took me out to meet the chairman of United Stationers. He told me this was a dumb idea. "Customers want better service," he said. "They don't want better prices. Forget it. It will never work. You'll fail." That's what he thought. But William Blair's venture fund invested in us, which helped us a lot, since a lot of the manufacturers were invested in it. And those manufacturers thought, You know, we ought to at least play with these guys, because it's probably gonna work, and we don't want to be left on the outside. Bessemer Venture Partners, another investor, happened to own Ampad, the big paper company out in Springfield, Mass. And because Bessemer was on the board of directors and called them up and said it was an investor in Staples, Ampad opened up to us, no questions asked, even though a lot of people were screaming at it.

We opened the first store, in Massachusetts, on May 1, 1986. By August, early September, we were getting lines at lunchtime. One of those days I came down from the office at lunchtime to help out. I started seeing lines at the register, and people talking about what a great deal they were getting. And you started seeing people who had driven down from Maine and up from Weymouth, Mass. That's when I started saying, "This could work."

Then Bain [& Co., the consultants], which did a lot of work for Avery Dennison, a wholesaler in the business, gave us a boost. They were telling their client, "We think the value channel will grow, and if you're smart, you'll partner up with Staples before your competitors do." They did, and it worked for them. Another break—it took a while, but the Canon guy finally agrees to send a sales rep up to come meet with me. I say, "Meet me at lunchtime." I take him to the store. It's a mob scene. And he just says, "I'll sell to you." About a year or two later, Hewlett-Packard puts this huge task force together—they decide they're gonna sell to us. And so one by one the dominoes fell.

At the time we had this one stinking store in Brighton, Mass. One day I'm walking around, shopping, and I recognize this guy. It's Joe Antonini, the CEO of Kmart. His industrial spies had reported to him there was this hot new business opening up there. Now if he is in my store, and I have one store in Brighton, this obviously has a whole lot more weight and more potential than even I think it does. I also heard a story from Charles Lazarus, CEO of Toys 'R' Us, that spring. He was on the Wal-Mart board. Each year the Wal-Mart executives have to identify the biggest new idea in retailing, the biggest threat to Wal-Mart—at least, Sam Walton used to do that in his day. And the executives report to the board. Lazarus reports to Robert Nakasone, a Toys 'R' Us executive who's also on my board, who says they reported that the biggest new idea in retailing is the Staples thing up in Massachusetts. And I said, "Oh, the jig is up. This is going to be a race." And sure enough, it turned out to be one.

> "WE HAD ONLY ONE MEASLY STORE OPEN WHEN KMART AND WAL-MART STARTED PAYING ATTENTION AND I THOUGHT, 'OH, NO, THE JIG IS UP.'"

From a value perspective, I think there's no question we've been a friend to the entrepreneur. If you look at the average small-town merchant, we've lowered the cost of his office products—where he was once paying, say, $4,000 or $5,000 a year, now he's paying $2,000 or $3,000. We made him more efficient. We made female entrepreneurs working out of the home more efficient. I'm sure we've had some deleterious side effects along the way too. Back in those days there were, I don't know, 15 major wholesalers. I think there are two today. There were 14,000 dealers. Today there are 6,000. But the positive benefit of what we've done for the productivity of small business and entrepreneurs lets me rest very comfortably in the confessional when I go.

Oh, yeah, the name. I'm driving between Hartford and Boston. I'm thinking about names. Pencils? Pens? 8 1/2-by-11? Staples? Staples! Staples the Office Superstore. That was it. The bad thing about the name was that when we started out, we had to explain to everybody what it was. Office Depot basically copied Home Depot and put the word "office" in front. It was a Home Depot for the office, and it lived off the Home Depot name. Office Club was a Price Club for the office. It lived off the Price Club name. In the early days ours was actually a problem. But those other names aren't brands. Ours is a brand."

II

Great
WAYS TO WORK

Techniques and Tips From
The Masters

GREAT WAYS TO WORK

Techniques and Tips From The Masters

He did his best work after dark, when the world was still and he could blow off steam on the office pipe organ. Around midnight Thomas Edison and his team would break for pie, ham, beer, and group sing-alongs. Refreshed by catnaps under his desk, the inventor would push himself and his dozen-plus researchers till dawn, when the sun finally reintroduced the concept of time. Clocks in the Menlo Park, N.J., laboratory stood still—Edison having removed their springs so that everything would revolve around his work. He would later say, "I owe my success to the fact that I never had a clock in my workroom."

You probably wouldn't want to copy Edison's methods—and even if you did, you probably wouldn't get the same results. (Although he did bequeath a practical benefit to workplaces everywhere: Burning the midnight oil no longer requires oil.) Yet the problem Edison solved is the one you still face: How do you make your work work for you?

It's not a question we're accustomed to asking ourselves—or others. So we sought out a variety of exceptionally effective people and practices. Here you'll discover how business icons and leaders answer the question. —*BY JERRY USEEM*

BEST-KEPT SECRETS OF THE WORLD'S BEST COMPANIES

By Paul Kaihla; Patrick Baltatzis; Harris Collingwood; Michael V. Copeland; Bridget Finn; Susanna Hamner; David Jacobson; Jeff Nachtigal; Erick Schonfeld; Paul Sloan; Owen Thomas

SECRET NO. 01:
Compare everything you do against your rivals. HP

EXTREME BENCHMARKING

HEWLETT-PACKARD CEO Mark Hurd loves numbers-and insists that his managers learn to love them too. Since Hurd came onboard in March 2005, one of the key tools he's used to keep pace with rivals is his extreme form of industry benchmarking. Instead of comparing HP's sales and profits with Dell's or IBM's, the company now tracks itself against rivals by every conceivable measure. "We want to make sure we break down every unit and business function," explains Marius Haas, senior strategy officer at HP, "so we can become best in class in each one."

Here's how it works: Imagine a matrix with various business units running down the side (printing, servers, storage, IT services, etc.) and business functions across the top (finance, HR, marketing, R&D, etc.). Now create benchmarks for each of the 72 resulting cells and you have a good idea of how Hurd is managing the $87 billion company. The benchmarks are the best guess of where HP's rivals are going to be in 2007, based on more than a dozen variables, from real estate cost per square foot to operating expenses as a percentage of gross margin.

Before Hurd took over, HP measured itself primarily against IBM, using one very blunt tool: costs as a percentage of revenues. That ignored IBM's higher gross margins and the fact that it has more gross profit to spread around. Hurd's new benchmarking method formed the basis of HP's reorganization effort announced in July 2005, through which HP has promised to save $3 billion by 2008. Already there is key evidence of success: Operating expenses as a percentage of gross margin dropped 2 percent in 2005, helping to fatten profits by $385 million. —*ERICK SCHONFELD*

SECRET NO. 02:
Create a lending library of ideas. IDEO

THE TECH BOX

Ideo helped create the Treo phone for Palm, the Leap chair for Steelcase, the stand-up toothpaste tube for Procter & Gamble, and hundreds of other products for top manufacturers. But there's one invention the Silicon Valley design shop keeps in-house: the "tech box," a freezer-size chest of drawers in each of its seven offices around the world. Inside each is the same library of up to 2,000 gadgets, materials, textiles, and artifacts that keep the creative gears of Ideo designers in constant motion. In drawers with labels like "thermal optical technologies," "amazing materials," and "cool mechanisms," designers can browse through everything from a swatch of fabric that glows in the dark to holographic candy, plywood tubes, and space-shuttle tiles.

"It's not a typical lending library," says Ideo designer Dennis Boyle, one of the company's principals and co-creator of the tech box along with Rickson Sun, Ideo's chief technologist. "People will pick out 20 items and bring them to a brainstorming session. We use the tech box to cross-pollinate every new project."

Take the Swiffer CarpetFlick, a recent Ideo project for P&G. During prototype tests, users gave the portable rug sweeper low marks for picking up carpet lint and other clingy materials. "The design team ran into a real roadblock," Boyle recalls. After a designer returned from the tech box with a lint brush, "we found that if we put a strip of it on the bottom of the Swiffer," Boyle says, "it rolled up lint in a way that gave it enough mass to be picked up by the scoop." The cheap fix helped support premium pricing: The CarpetFlick now sells for $12.99. —*PAUL KAIHLA*

SECRET NO. 03:
Appoint official devil's advocates to challenge the merits of deals. TORO

THE CONTRA TEAM

The appetite for mergers only gets bigger: U.S. companies consummated an estimated $1 trillion worth of M&A deals in 2005, up from $781 billion in 2004. All this despite the grim reality: Two-thirds of all acquisitions fail to meet their goals, according to a study by Booz Allen Hamilton.

Toro, the $1.8 billion lawn-mower giant, knows how to curb the urge to merge. Anytime an M&A pitch reaches the desk of CEO Mike Hoffman, he asks a due-diligence group to make the case to the company's board. But he also turns to the "contra team"—half a dozen vice presidents and directors—to deliver the voice of dissent. According to chairman Ken Melrose, who got the idea from reading about a similar practice at Japanese firms, a few years ago the contras killed an eight-figure acquisition of a manufacturer that had pitched itself as a turnaround success. The contras' number crunching showed that its sector was facing a slump. The prospect's revenues have since tanked, while Toro has nearly doubled its sales. "Naysaying in corporate America isn't popular," Melrose says. "The contra team is a way to create negative views that are in the shareholders' best interest and the company's best interest."—*PAUL KAIHLA*

SECRET NO. 04:
Use office design to keep the queen in touch with the worker bees. Bloomberg

THE CORPORATE BEEHIVE

Bloomberg's new Lexington Avenue headquarters in Manhattan is more than just architectural shock and awe. Its centerpiece—a courtyard enclosed by a six-story elliptical "curtain" of tubular steel and glass—resembles a cross section of a beehive, with workers exposed on each level. Modeled after the trading floors where founder Michael Bloomberg got his start, the building is a wide-open expanse of workspaces devoid of private offices and cubicles. Even the conference rooms have glass walls.

CEO Lex Fenwick, who sits at an open desk on the sixth floor surrounded by some 125 sales and customer service staffers, doesn't mind the praise he's received for the striking design. What he cares about most, though, is the view he has from the catbird seat. "I know quicker than any piece of damn software when we have a problem. I can see it right in front of me when it happens," Fenwick says. "I watch the phone calls; I see the stress level on faces. Someone can look at me and say, 'We've got a problem.' What does it allow me to do? Get on someone to fix it in seconds. The communication this setup affords is staggering." —*PAUL KAIHLA*

SECRET NO. 05:
Keep a constant eye out for trouble. CP

BAD NEWS FOLDERS
Business was good at Colgate-Palmolive during the 1990s—so good that CEO Reuben Mark began worrying about what might go wrong. So he decided to install an early-warning system to flag problems before they blew up into company-wrecking crises. Each day at Colgate, half a dozen or so clear red plastic folders land on the CEO's desk, as well as the desks of other top execs. Inside each is a "situation report," a form that regional managers fill out to describe brewing trouble of any sort—from factory slowdowns to worker injuries. On a recent day, one folder mentioned the robbery of one of the company's delivery trucks in the Dominican Republic. Another reported the discovery of counterfeit toothpaste tubes in a South African market.

Local managers handled those issues. But when a report alerted Mark that officials in Baddi, India, had questions about how a plant treated wastewater, Colgate quickly involved an engineering team to avoid potential embarrassment. Another perk of the process? Its self-policing power. "No one is going to report a problem," a company executive says, "and then not do anything about it. You can say it's boring, but process does make the world go around." —*HARRIS COLLINGWOOD*

SECRET NO. 06:
Bring in experts to help spark new ideas. CORNING

OUTSIDE-IN R&D
In 2006 Corning will spend about $450 million—some 10 percent of its revenues—on research and development. And it will also realize the fruits of such lavish spending, with plans to launch dozens of high-tech products, from a new diesel emissions technology to exotic green lasers. But the company's new-product pipeline doesn't begin and end with R&D. Rather than relying solely on scientists toiling in the labs, Corning regularly teams up its workers with entrepreneurs and big thinkers from outside the company to come up with ideas for new products.

A few times a year, the company runs half-day brainstorm sessions at its New York headquarters to kick off the quest for innovations. First, managers from a special marketing group—a 15-person unit tasked with identifying $500 million-plus business opportunities-gather for several hours to listen to outside experts, from renewable energy gurus to nanotech engineers.

The group then breaks into teams of five, each assigned to drum up ideas related to the talk. After that, the most promising ideas are handed off to teams of two employees: one with a marketing background, the other with technical expertise. ("We find great constructive conflict this way," says Deborah Mills, head of the early-stage marketing team.) The two spend up to four months hashing out feasibility and market potential, and then present the plan to execs, who give it the go-ahead or send it back for more research. In October 2004, one team devised a method for making water desalinization faster and cheaper, using carbon electrodes. Up to $74 million has been set aside to bring that project, and several others, to market. —*BRIDGET FINN*

SECRET NO. 07:
Take no stake until you earn it. HONEST TEA

EQUITY AS YOU GO

Since its launch in 1998, Honest Tea has become the top bottled- organic-tea brand in the United States. Sales have climbed an average of 65 percent per year, and revenues recently hit $10 million. What's its special brew? A funding formula gave the founders zero equity until they doubled the company's value.

Honest Tea chairman Barry Nalebuff, a Yale business school professor, and president Seth Goldman, his former student, figured there was a more honest way to get funding than to make wild guesses about future sales. So they proposed a plan to investors whereby they would earn equity in the company only after raising the value of shares by multiples of two, three, five, ten, and 15. "We said, 'We don't know what Honest Tea is worth,'" Nalebuff says, "but we'll give you the whole thing until we double your money."

Within a few weeks, the pair landed $500,000 to get Honest Tea started. One hundred shares in the company, valued at $5,000 apiece, were split among several investors. In early 2006 shares in the privately held company were worth $42,000 each, and Nalebuff and Goldman have- deservedly-earned their current 25 percent stake. —*PAUL KAIHLA*

SECRET NO. 08:
Turn the interview process into an all-encompassing tryout. SOUTHWEST

THE JOB AUDITION

You don't just get interviewed when you apply for a job at Southwest Airlines. You get auditioned—and it starts the moment you call for an application.

Given that ultrafriendly service is critical to the $7.6 billion carrier's success, it's little wonder that HR managers don't wait until the interview to start screening. When a candidate calls for an application, managers jot down anything memorable about the conversation, good or bad. The same is true when the company flies recruits out for interviews. They receive special tickets, which alert gate agents, flight attendants, and others to pay special attention: Are they friendly to others or griping about service and slurping cocktails at 8 a.m.? If what the employees observe seems promising—or not—they're likely to pass it on to HR.

Even when recruits aren't on the spot, they're on the spot. During group interviews of flight attendants, applicants take turns giving three-minute speeches about themselves in front of as many as 50 others. The catch? Managers are watching the audience as closely as the speaker. Candidates who pay attention pass the test; those who seem bored or distracted get bounced. "We want to see how they interact with people when they think they're not being evaluated," says Southwest recruiter Michael Burkhardt. The screening method not only keeps turnover low (about 5.5 percent annually) but keeps customers happy. Every year since 1987, the carrier has received the lowest number of passenger complaints in the industry. —*MICHAEL V. COPELAND*

SECRET NO. 09:
Turn going-through-the-motions meetings into no-holds-barred debates. P&G

STRATEGIC STRATEGY REVIEWS

Since A.G. Lafley became CEO of Procter & Gamble in 2000, the company's portfolio of billion-dollar brands has swelled from ten to 17 and sales have jumped from $40 billion to more than $57 billion. So what's behind the good-to-great transformation? Lafley chalks it up to the way the company conducts annual strategy reviews—the all-day powwows that set the tone and direction for every product.

When Lafley arrived, the reviews were more theater than

debate. Division presidents would march to the podium, click through pre-approved PowerPoint slides, and wait for the execs to rubber-stamp the plan. The problem? "They were justifying why bad performance wasn't so bad if you looked at it properly," says Roger Martin, an adviser to Lafley and dean of the University of Toronto's Rotman School of Management. "And they had thick briefing books to back that up."

So Lafley junked the old agenda and installed a new one. First, he asks each division head to send the presentation to him before the formal review. He sends it back with a handful of key concerns to concentrate on at the gathering. (Presenters are limited to three pages to save time for questions.) Second, the reviews don't wrap up by 5 p.m.; the process can last days or weeks until everyone agrees. Third, Lafley focuses each debate around two objectives: "where to play" and "how to win." According to Martin, the bare-knuckles review process is responsible for Pampers's recent market-share gains over Kimberly-Clark's Huggies. Lafley and other execs helped division president Deb Henretta plot "where to play" (in the more profitable training-pants segment instead of regular diapers) and "how to win" (attacking Pampers's cost structure so that P&G could better match its rival's prices). "When we get it right," Lafley says, "we can boil it down into a one-page document that provides clarity for everyone-and more consistent execution." —*PAUL KAIHLA*

SECRET NO. 10:
Let employees choose their leaders. GORE

PEER-TO-PEER PROMOTION
The invention in the mid-1970s of wonder fabric Gore-Tex, an off-shoot of W.L. Gore's development of high-speed computer cables, put the Delaware-based company on the map. But the successes that have come since that breakthrough—including Glide dental floss and high-end Elixir guitar strings-owe more to the company's grassroots management structure than to high-tech R&D.

Except for a handful of top executives, all 6,800 employees

have the same title: associate. From there, upward mobility follows an unusual path. Some associates act as "sponsors" to help pair colleagues' interests to particular projects. If you want to become a "team leader," you don't lobby the higher-ups for a promotion; you form an alliance of people willing to commit to a specific goal, whether it's pitching a product or a new health plan. Beyond the egalitarian appeal, the org structure helps ideas bubble up faster than they might through conventional R&D. Elixir strings, for example, came about after engineering associate Dave Myers wondered whether the hard coating on cables might make guitar strings more durable. He paired up with a musician colleague, and the company green-lighted the project. Today, Elixir has become the top-selling acoustic guitar string in the United States. And worker turnover at Gore averages 5 percent annually, far lower than the manufacturing industry average of 13 percent. —*HARRIS COLLINGWOOD*

SECRET NO. 11:
Reward workers for keeping their hands off the merchandise. MEN'S WEARHOUSE

THE SHRINK SHRINKER

"Shrink"—not to be confused with the Seinfeld term "shrinkage"—is nonetheless a mortifying issue for retailers. The term refers to the percentage of inventory that goes missing between audits (mostly as a result of employee theft), a problem that cost U.S. companies an estimated $31 billion in 2005.

Men's Wearhouse has a novel method for shrinking the shrink. The $1.7 billion retailer pays managers quarterly bonuses when stores report shrink levels deemed good or excellent. Company president Charlie Bresler declines to share exact figures, except to say that "good" means below industry average and "excellent" means "well below." The bonuses, he says, are "more than a couple hundred bucks, but not enough to buy a car." Of course, it's not all about the cash, he says: The bonuses reinforce the notion that "when workers steal from you, they are stealing from themselves and their colleagues." —*MICHAEL V. COPELAND*

SECRET NO. 12:
Determine pay using just two factors: profits and seniority. Egon Zehnder International

THE ANTI-STAR SYSTEM

Despite having 900 employees in 38 countries, Egon Zehnder, the world's fourth-largest headhunting firm, keeps no records of billable hours and doesn't hand out a cent in commissions or bonuses. Compensation for its 300 or so partners is determined by two variables alone: seniority and corporate profits.

Here's how it works. When consultants are elected to be partners (usually after five years), they become shareholders, with each owning an equal slice of the company. For up to 15 years, partners also earn one "seniority point" per year, each worth a small percentage of annual profits. The system "guarantees total collaboration," explains Dan Meiland, the company's New York-based executive chairman. "No one has to ask for favors. The only way people can increase the profit pie is by helping colleagues please their clients. We want new consultants to be better than the old ones because it's the only way to increase the profit pool. So the talent pool is always upgraded." The company's 2005 profits were estimated at more than $100 million. —*PAUL KAIHLA*

SECRET NO. 13:
Use prediction markets to tap hidden knowledge. Microsoft

A NEW OFFICE POOL

If so-called prediction markets—betting pools in which shares are traded to gauge the odds of upcoming events—can call presidential elections and Oscar races with accuracy, why not use them inside companies to identify their next hit products? The answer: It's a lot harder to tap into collective brainpower about a product's market potential, and other key business questions, than it is to foretell the winner for Best Picture.

Microsoft, though, is trying to crack the code—and has been developing prediction markets as a serious alternative to blunt forecasting tools. Todd Proebsting, director of Microsoft's Center for Software Excellence, began running a series of prediction markets in 2004 to better gauge how many bugs a new software application might contain and to make more accurate calls about product ship dates. In his first effort, Proebsting chose 25 programmers and quality-control testers from a team of more than 50 working on a new Windows testing application. Via an internal website, workers could buy shares for the month they believed the product would ship. Shares were valued at $1 apiece, and the engineers drew on accounts stocked with $50 each to fund their bids. Within minutes of the site's launch, shares for a February ship date shot up in value while those for November, the scheduled release date, dropped to almost zero. That came as a shock to the project director, who had heard nothing but optimism in meetings and e-mail updates.

Exposing such communication gaps gives prediction markets even more potential value to businesses, Proebsting says. "Face-to-face communication breaks down, and opinions are filtered," he says. "Prediction markets show where the gap is and allow you to short-circuit it." In this case, the project manager did more troubleshooting ahead of time and avoided a delivery crisis. On the strength of those results, Proebsting ran another two dozen markets on a variety of software projects. Each, he says, accurately predicted the completion date. What's next, then, for this nascent technology in Redmond? Daniel Ling, chief of Microsoft Research, will say only that it's something the company "continues to explore." —*PAUL KAIHLA*

SECRET NO. 14:
Let workers speak their minds. Google

OFFICE GRAFFITI
For a company that has roughly doubled its workforce each year since 2002 (headcount in early 2006: 5,800), Google does-

n't much act like the big company it has become. One of the ways it has preserved its tech-startup ethos is decidedly low-tech: dozens of whiteboards placed in common areas and corridors throughout its Mountain View, Calif., campus. Some are businesslike, used by product teams to swap ideas. But the two largest ones, about 30 feet long, are devoted to the equivalent of corporate graffiti. One is packed with cartoons and jokes that workers have scrawled under the slogan "Google's Plan for World Domination." "It's collaborative art," says David Krane, Google's director of communications and one of its earliest whiteboard posters. "We're in a growth period, and when new hires see the boards, they get a quick, comprehensive snapshot of our personality." —*Paul Kaihla*

SECRET NO. 15:
Use kickbacks—the legal kind— to attract executive talent. SAIC

THE PYRAMID SCHEME

It's a far cry from selling soap, but $7.2 billion defense contractor SAIC has for years stolen a page from Amway in the way it recruits and rewards top executives. When certain managers land a new contract, they get a bonus. Then a cut gets passed up to their boss, and their boss's boss. The practice creates incentives for VPs and directors to recruit high earners instead of cronies and is credited with helping SAIC to achieve 33 consecutive years of sales growth through 2002.

In a traditional pyramid-sales model, people at the top skim from the newest and lowest hires. SAIC's pyramid involves only a few layers in the upper half of the org chart. While the company confirms that the practice continues today, it declines to elaborate on the details. —*Paul Kaihla*

SECRET NO. 16:
Keep retirees in the labor pool. INTEL

THE LONG GOODBYE

Forget gold watches and engraved plaques. When workers at Intel retire, they get a strangely utilitarian going-away present: a laptop or PC (Intel inside, of course), along with a printer, free Internet access, tech support, and—most important—invitations to quarterly briefings with senior executives about the company's performance and new products.

If that sounds almost like a job, you're onto Intel's scheme. "They're part of the family, and you want to keep them in it as much as possible," says Tom Galvin, Intel's director of compensation and benefits. More important, Intel wants to keep retirees available for consulting work, since demographic trends predict that demand for skilled workers will soar during the next couple of decades. Today, Intel's senior talent pool stands at about 1,200. Says Galvin: "We want them to stick around for when things get tight." —*PAUL KAIHLA*

SECRET NO. 17:
Let your customers do the marketing. Mozilla

OPEN-SOURCE AD CAMPAIGNS

In the 18 months after Mozilla released its open-source Firefox browser in 2004, more than 150 million users downloaded it. Not bad, considering the nonprofit foundation has no marketing staff to speak of.

So what keeps Firefox hot? SpreadFirefox.com, a Mozilla website where users post ideas for marketing schemes and volunteers put the most popular ideas into action. Don't laugh: The site has more than 160,000 members, and Mozilla claims it has lured 10 million users away from other browsers.

Last year one fan suggested a series of online greeting cards that included a Firefox link. Graphic designers signed up to create dozens of e-cards, which triggered thousands of downloads. Next came a feature that invites fans to record 30-second video ads and post them to a gallery for viewing. (Think of Apple's "Switch" campaign, minus the Hollywood budget.) This month a panel will vote on the best, and the winner gets $5,000, donated by electronics retailer B&H.

The genius behind it all? Mozilla staffer Asa Dotzler pitched it to Firefox co-creator Blake Ross, who says the site is "one of our superhigh-return-on-investment projects." Dotzler, 32, became SpreadFirefox's community coordinator. —*PAUL KAIHLA*

SECRET NO. 18:
Turn employees into trend-spotters. Urban Outfitters

LATE-NIGHT RECON
Finding the next big thing isn't just the job of Urban Outfitters's designers and buyers. The $1 billion retailer counts on everyone from store managers to interns to help it stay ahead of the curve. In return for free concert tickets and nights on the town, workers "communicate what is seen and heard back to the buying and design teams," says merchandise manager Laura O'Connor. The eyes-and-ears tactic has led to hit products, she adds. So who do they keep the closest tabs on? That's the one thing she won't share: "I'd rather not give the folks we shadow cause for keeping us at arm's length."—*SUSANNA HAMNER*

SECRET NO. 19:
Head off shareholder trouble before it starts. Coca-Cola

THE CHIEF SHAREHOLDER OFFICER
When you're a multibillion-dollar household name, it can take more than shareholder meetings and proxy mailings to keep thousands of investors in the loop—or from stirring up unnecessary trouble. One of the few public companies to make investor relations something more than just an extension of PR is $23 billion Coca-Cola. Mark Preisinger, Coke's director of shareowner affairs since 1999, is considered the top-ranking investor-relations chief in the United States. Not because of his title, but because of his clout and independence from the CEO.

Unlike his counterparts at the vast majority of public companies, Preisinger reports directly to Coke's general counsel, not to CEO Neville Isdell, and relays investor concerns straight to the company's board. That's a tough job at Coke, which is a constant target of activist shareholder resolutions. Many stray far outside the realm of day to day business, demanding everything from an investigation of antiunion violence in Colombia to a review of Coke's impact on the AIDS and avian flu crises. "When most companies get hit with these resolutions, they adopt a bunker mentality and never call the shareholders who file them," says Nell Minow, a top corporate governance critic and co-founder of the Corporate Library. "Mark calls all of the people who file resolutions, and he often gets them to withdraw the resolution."

And when he can't, on more substantive issues? He pushes both sides to broker a deal. Preisinger recently spent 12 months working with the International Brotherhood of Teamsters General Fund, which demanded a cap on executive severance packages. In 2005 the board signed the deal, limiting severance to three times annual salary and bonuses. —*BRIDGET FINN*

SECRET NO. 20:
Start each day with a lightning-fast, all-hands briefing. UPS

THE THREE-MINUTE HUDDLE
How does UPS keep 220,000 drivers and package handlers on time? Wireless transmitters, reliable trucks, and a world-class logistics network are critical, of course. But managers have their own safeguard against slack. Every morning, and often several times per day, managers gather workers for a mandatory meeting that lasts precisely three minutes.

The talks start with company announcements, from benefits updates to bulletins about software upgrades on drivers' handhelds. Then managers go over local information: traffic conditions or customer complaints. Every meeting ends with a safety tip.

The meetings ensure that workers are always kept in the

loop, and the 180-second limit helps enforce system-wide punc-tuality. If drivers are late to start their routes because meetings run long, they'll earn overtime pay and deliver fewer packages-exactly what UPS strives to avoid. The practice has proven so successful that many hourly office workers now start their days with a three-minute huddle of their own. —OWEN THOMAS

SECRET NO. 21:
Get the directors out of the boardroom. The Home Depot

ALWAYS-ON BOARD MEMBERS

At $82 billion home-improvement king Home Depot, corpo-rate governance is practically a full-time job. Eager to keep the directors better in tune with the company's operations—and less dependent on chairman and CEO Bob Nardelli for their intelligence—five years ago Nardelli began requiring all 12 board members to make daylong visits to a dozen stores a year and relay their findings to the board.

Directors choose the stores they visit (typically dropping in unannounced) and go into action. In the parking lot, they chat with customers about what they like and don't. Inside, they do the same with managers and staff, and also do spot checks of cus-tomer service and inventory assortment. At quarterly board meet-ings, the agenda always includes time to discuss the field trips.

The reconnaissance missions aren't just a public-relations ploy. In fact, the Corporate Library's Minow considers the practice a rare exemplar. "It's not good for directors to operate in a closed loop and only get information from the CEO," she says. "It's the differ-ence between examining store shelves and reading a PowerPoint." The program also helps weed out directors who aren't up to the task: Two Home Depot board members have resigned since 2004, in part because they couldn't make the time. —BRIDGET FINN

SECRET NO. 22:
Seek brutally honest feedback from customers. Medtronic

SURGICAL VISITS

Aloof. Arrogant. Inwardly focused. That's how Bill George recalls customers describing Medtronic when he became CEO of the $10 billion medical-device maker in 1991. So George set out to change the perceptions. During his first month on the job, he watched a surgeon perform an angioplasty using a new Medtronic balloon catheter. As the device was fed through an artery, it disintegrated. In a fury, the surgeon flung the bloody mess at George, who avoided a direct hit.

A perfect opportunity, it turned out, to make some changes. Chastened, George made sure that an improved catheter hit the market within three months. Then he began requiring all engineers and designers to attend one surgical procedure a year to see Medtronic products in action. Their presence not only gives surgeons a chance to vent, the company claims it gets new product ideas just from watching. "Observing helps to constantly improve product design," says George, who retired in 2002, "because the customer is never going to be completely satisfied." —*HARRIS COLLINGWOOD*

SECRET NO. 23:
Pass cost savings on to those who achieved them.
Whole Foods Market

GAINSHARING

At $4.7 billion Whole Foods Market, when store department "teams" finish a four-week period under their payroll budget, the company doesn't keep the surplus. Rather, it gets handed down to the employees whose efficiency created the savings.

Here's how it works. Managers constantly track their payroll spending against their budget. Every four weeks they divide any surplus by the hours logged and add the result, or "gainshare," to workers' hourly wages. If the surplus is $2,000, on 1,200 hours, each employee gets an extra $1.67 per hour. The company claims the incentive not only pushes workers to step it up a notch but also aids in recruiting. Newcomers need a two-thirds vote from colleagues to be brought on permanently. As company spokeswoman Amy Schaefer notes, "It's a chance for team members to say, 'This person is not catching on, they're not productive,' because they're going to share their gainsharing with them." —*DAVID JACOBSON*

SECRET NO. 24:
Neutralize your customers' worst fears. Honda

THE "JUST LOOKING" BADGE
Car shopping as entertainment has always been the draw at Planet Honda in Union, N.J., one of Honda's fastest-growing dealerships. A giant video wall shows footage of the latest models, and new-car buyers get a G-force ride on an 18-foot spaceship simulator. The best part of the show? The "tech cafe," where the presence of salespeople is strictly verboten, and where a receptionist asks shoppers if they need help. If you respond the way most do—"Just looking, thanks"—you get a yellow smiley—face badge emblazoned with the letters "JL" to stick on your lapel, which alerts the sales guys to back off.

Not for long. Planet Honda owner Tim Ciasulli says JLs turn out to be his best customers, because the badge helps to lower their defenses. "The magic is when they peel it off after 15 minutes and they're ready to do business," Ciasulli says. The dealership sold 3,300 new cars in 2005, more than three times the average for independent dealerships. —*PAUL KAIHLA*

SECRET NO. 25:
Become your own customer. Guitar Center

PHONE SHOPPING
When the phone rings at any of Guitar Center's 165 stores, the salespeople are expected to pick it up before the fourth ring— especially if the manager happens to be off at one of the company's motivational sessions. That's because the off-sites include a kind of hazing ritual called "phone shopping" that

keeps store workers on their toes. At past meetings, held three times a year at a rock club near the company's Southern California headquarters, it's worked like this: A woman in a tight skirt stands on the stage spinning a container of ping-pong balls, each representing a Guitar Center outlet. When a ball pops up, the lucky store manager is called up to the stage while a company executive calls the store. The exec not only checks that the clerk on the other end answers the phone quickly, but then grills him about the company's core principles or techniques for closing a deal. The entire conversation is broadcast over the PA system for all the other managers to hear. "It's brutal—a complete public flogging—but very effective," says Maxx Galster, who got his start on the sales floor and now oversees the chain's store operations. "You really see the truth come out." —*PAUL SLOAN*

HOW I WORK

By Bill Gates

It's pretty incredible to look back 30 years to when Microsoft was starting and realize how work has been transformed. We're finally getting close to what I call the digital work-style.

If you look at this office, there isn't much paper in it. On my desk I have three screens, synchronized to form a single desktop. I can drag items from one screen to the next. Once you have that large display area, you'll never go back, because it has a direct impact on productivity. The screen on the left has my list of e-mails. On the center screen is usually the specific e-mail I'm reading and responding to. And my browser is on the right-hand screen. This setup gives me the ability to glance and see what new has come in while I'm working on something, and to bring up a link that's related to an e-mail and look at it while the e-mail is still in front of me.

At Microsoft, e-mail is the medium of choice, more than phone calls, documents, blogs, bulletin boards, or even meetings (voicemails and faxes are actually integrated into our e-mail in-boxes). I get about 100 e-mails a day. We apply filtering to keep it to that level—e-mail comes straight to me from anyone I've ever corresponded with, anyone from Microsoft, Intel, HP, and all the other partner companies, and anyone I know. And I always see a write-up from my assistant of any other e-mail, from companies that aren't on my permission list or individuals I don't know. That way I know what people are praising us for, what they are complaining about, and what they are asking.

We're at the point now where the challenge isn't how to communicate effectively with e-mail, it's ensuring that you spend your time on the e-mail that matters most. I use tools like "in-box rules" and search folders to mark and group messages based on their content and importance. I'm not big on to-do lists. Instead, I use e-mail and desktop folders and my online calendar. So when I walk up to my desk, I can focus on the e-mails I've flagged and check the folders that are monitoring particular projects and particular blogs.

Outlook also has a little notification box that comes up in the lower right whenever a new e-mail comes in. We call it "the toast." I'm very disciplined about ignoring that unless I see that it's a high-priority topic.

Staying focused is one issue; that's the problem of information overload. The other problem is information underload. Being flooded with information doesn't mean we have the right information or that we're in touch with the right people. I deal with this by using SharePoint, a tool that creates websites for collaboration on specific projects. These sites contain plans, schedules, discussion boards, and other information, and they can be created by just about anyone in the company with a couple of clicks.

Right now, I'm getting ready for Think Week. I regularly go off for a week and read 100 or more papers from Microsoft employees that examine issues related to the company and the future of technology. I've been doing this for over 12 years. It used to be an all-paper process in which I was the only one doing the reading and commenting. Today the whole process is digital and open to the entire company. I'm now far more efficient in picking the right papers to read, and I can add electronic comments that everyone sees in real time.

Microsoft has more than 50,000 people, so when I'm thinking, "Hey, what's the future of the online payment system?" or "What's a great way to keep track of your memories of your kid?" or any neat new thing, I write it down. Then people can see it and say, "No, you're wrong" or "Did you know about this work being done at such-and-such a place?" SharePoint puts me in touch with lots of people deep in the organization. It's like having a super-website that lets many people edit and discuss far more than the standard practice of sending e-mails with enclosures. And it notifies you if anything comes up in an area you're interested in.

Another digital tool that has had a big effect on my productivity is desktop search. It has transformed the way I access information on my PC, on servers, and on the Internet. With larger hard drives and increasing bandwidth, I now have gigabytes of information on my PC and servers in the form of e-mails, documents, media files, contact databases, and so on. Instead of having to navigate through folders to find that one document where I think a piece of information might be, I simply type search terms into a toolbar, and all the e-mails and documents that contain that information are at my fingertips. The same goes for phone numbers and e-mail addresses. Paper is no longer a big part of my day. I get 90 percent of my news online, and when I go to a meeting and want to jot things down, I bring my Tablet PC. It's fully synchronized with my office machine so I have all the files I need. It also has a note-taking piece of software called OneNote, so all my notes are in digital form.

The one low-tech piece of equipment still in my office is my whiteboard. I always have nice color pens, and it's great for brainstorming when I'm with other people, and even sometimes by myself. The whiteboards in some Microsoft offices have the ability to capture an image and send it up to the computer, almost like a huge Tablet PC. I don't have that right now, but probably I'll get a digital whiteboard in the next year. Today, if there's something up there that's brilliant, I just get out my pen and my Tablet PC and re-create it.

"PAPER ISN'T A BIG PART OF MY DAY"
—BILL GATES, *chairman and chief software architect, Microsoft U.S.A*

Days are often filled with meetings. It's a nice luxury to get some time to go write up my thoughts or follow up on meetings during the day. But sometimes that doesn't happen. So then it's great after the kids go to bed to be able to just sit at home and go through whatever e-mail I didn't get to. If the entire week is very busy, it's the weekend when I'll send the long, thoughtful pieces of e-mail. When people come in Monday morning, they'll see that I've been quite busy—they'll have a lot of e-mail.

SUPER-ACHIEVERS: HOW THEY STAY AHEAD IN THE FAST LANE

By: Alex Taylor III; David Kirkpatrick; Andy Serwer; Jon Birger; Ellen McGirt; Roger Parloff; Jia Lynn Yang; Ellen McGirt; Devin Leonard; Roger Parloff; Patricia Sellers

Carlos Ghosn,
CEO of Renault (France) and Nissan (Japan)

Focus relentlessly.

I go from Paris to Tokyo every month and spend between one and two weeks there. The week when I am in Tokyo is the week when I have the Nissan executive committee meeting, the design meeting, the product decision meeting, the investment meeting, the board meeting—all the important meetings are taking place during this week. I do the same thing at Renault. To put decisions into action, I hand them to the executive committee.

Every month is different. In March of 2006, I will be one week in the U.S. (I'm also head of Nissan's North American operations), one week in Japan, two weeks in France. But everybody knows that the first week of the month I am in Paris and the third week of the month I'm in Japan.

I have an assistant in France, one in Japan, and one in the U.S. They are all bilingual: Japanese and English, French and English. My assistants screen all the mail and documents. I'm very selective. They know exactly the topics I am interested in and what should be diverted to other members of the executive committee. For meetings on a single topic that aren't regular operational meetings, I'm very strict. The maximum is one hour and 30 minutes. Fifty percent of the time is for the presentation, 50 percent is for discussion.

I do my best thinking early in the morning. I always ask that my first meeting not happen before eight. When I need more time to think, I wake up earlier. If I don't do six hours of sleep, I'm in bad shape, but I'm usually up by six.

The risk in holding two jobs is that you are going to lose some details. We have organized ourselves in a way where I still see many, many people in both companies, so I consider myself in really good contact with reality. Some things I have to sacrifice. When I was in Japan running Nissan, I used to visit one dealer a month and one plant every two or three months. Now dealer visits are once every six months, and plants are once every year.

It is also important to take a distance from the problem. I do not bring my work home. I play with my four children and spend time with my family on weekends. When I go to work on Monday, I can look at the problem with more distance. I come up with good ideas as a result of becoming stronger after being recharged.

Stress builds up when you know that there is a problem, but you do not clearly see it, and you do not have a solution. We're all human. I want to assure you I feel the same pain and the same stress and the same jet lag as anybody else. You have nights when you cannot sleep, and the stress is unbearable. It happens to every single person in a job like this. —*INTERVIEWED BY ALEX TAYLOR III*

Marissa Mayer,
VP, Search Products and User Experience, Google

Don't just cope with information—revel in it.

I don't feel overwhelmed with information. I really like it. I use Gmail for my personal e-mail—15 to 20 e-mails a day—but on my work e-mail I get as many as 700 to 800 a day, so I need something really fast. I use an e-mail application called Pine, a Linux-based utility I started using in college. It's a very simple text-based mailer in a crunchy little terminal window with Courier fonts. You can log onto the server directly, so you don't have the

> **"I'LL JUST SIT DOWN AND DO E-MAIL FOR TEN TO 14 HOURS STRAIGHT."**
> —MARISSA MAYER, *Google*

"headers are now downloading" problem that you do in client applications like Outlook. I do marathon e-mail catch-up sessions, sometimes on a Saturday or Sunday. I'll just sit down and do e-mail for ten to 14 hours straight. I almost always have the radio or my TV on. Sometimes it's the news. Sometimes it's a sitcom. I actually like the two streams of information. I guess I'm a typical 25- to 35-year-old who's now really embracing the two-screen experience.

I'm very speed-sensitive. With TiVo, for example, I just seem to spend too much of my life looking at the PLEASE WAIT sign. I adore my cellphone, but there's just a second of delay when you answer it: Hello, hello? I do have a BlackBerry. I don't use it at work because we have wireless throughout the office. I like my laptop a lot more, especially now that I have an EVDO [broadband cellular] card that gives me online access almost everywhere.

I almost always have my laptop with me. It's sitting with me right now. We are a very laptop-friendly culture. It's not uncommon to walk into a meeting at Google where everyone has a laptop open. One caveat is that [chairman and CEO] Eric Schmidt has a large aversion to sitting next to somebody who's typing, so we advise people who want to have a good experience in a meeting with Eric not to bring their laptop.

To keep track of tasks, I have a little document called a task list. And in the same document there's a list for each person I work with or interact with, of what they're working on or what I expect from them. It's just a list in a text file. Using this, I can plan my day out the night before: "These are the five high-priority things to focus on." But at Google things can change pretty fast. This morning I had my list of what I thought I was going to do today, but now I'm doing entirely different things.

I've been trying to figure out how to make time that was previously unproductive productive. If I'm driving my car somewhere, I try to get a call in to my family and friends then. Or during dead time when I'm waiting in line, I will hop on my cellphone and get something done.

My day starts around 9 a.m. and meetings finish up around 8 p.m. After that I stay in the office to do action items and e-mail. I can get by on four to six hours of sleep. I pace myself by taking a weeklong vacation every four months.

I have an assistant, Patty, who handles calls from the outside, answers e-mails, letters, and requests. She does a great job with scheduling. In an average week I'm getting scheduled into about 70 meetings, probably ten or 11 hours a day. On Friday, Patty lets me out early—around 6, and I go up to San Francisco and do something interesting.

From 4 to 5:30 every day that I can, I'll sit at my desk to answer any question that shows up on my doorstep. We have a big sign-up sheet outside. We joke that we should get one of those deli number tickers—"Now serving No. 68!" But we have nice couches and power for laptops and things outside the door where people wait. The average seems to be around 13 people per day. Sometimes they show me mockups or new demos of ideas they want to advance. Sometimes they have a presentation they're working on. Or sometimes they just want to ask me a question about Google's overall management. Anything is fair game. So if they ask, "Why are we in China?" I try to answer as candidly as I can. —*INTERVIEWED BY DAVID KIRKPATRICK*

Howard Schultz,

Chairman, Starbucks

Rise early—and have the occasional jolt of joe.

I get up between 5 and 5:30, and naturally the first thing I do is make some coffee; depending on my mood, it's either an espresso macchiato or one of our Indonesian coffees in a French press. I'll take my coffee, read three newspapers—the *Seattle Times*, *The Wall Street Journal*, and *The New York Times*—and listen to a voicemail summarizing sales results from the past 24 hours. This has been my routine for 25 years.

There are always Starbucks with their lights on somewhere around the globe, and we open five new stores every day. So I've learned how to leverage my time. In the early morning I focus on Europe. I'll call Greece or Spain or wherever, either at home or on the drive into work, to talk about challenges—do the numbers make sense?—or to congratulate them. These personal conversations are very important.

At work the first thing I do is read the flash report, which is our roadmap of what we do that day. We manage day-to-day in our business. I'm proud that we are so nimble—we have great information flow to make that happen. So we attend to U.S. business during the day, and of course at night I'll be speaking with Asia.

I'm always stopping by our stores—at least 25 a week. I'm also in other places: Home Depot, Whole Foods, Crate & Barrel. I was just in a great [home improvement] store, Tokyu Hands, in Tokyo; it's fun and it grabs you. I try to be a sponge to pick up as much as I can. I'm traveling internationally now one out of every seven weeks. China is going to be very significant for us, and it's something I've been spearheading. The travel can be brutal—I got back from China five days ago, and I'm still a little under the weather. The airplane is my time to read, which I do voraciously. I carry a Treo powered by GoodLink, which works well globally. I'm not a big e-mailer, though; it's a crutch that hinders person-to-person communication. I don't really have any secret tools or books or tricks—other than I could always use a good cup of coffee. —*INTERVIEWED BY ANDY SERWER*

Bill Gross,
Chief Investment Officer, Pimco

Cut through the noise.

I get up about 4:30 a.m. and check out the markets. I have a Bloomberg and a Telerate and some other machines downstairs. Bloomberg is the most important: You can get a review of the most recent New York play or you can get a 50-year currency history of the Brazilian *real*. It's amazing what you can access. Anyway, I check out Japan and Europe. I make myself some breakfast and then head off to work about 5:45 a.m. and get into the office about 6.

The first hour or two is used for acclimating to the markets and various economic data releases. Lots of big, macro numbers—GDP, the unemployment number, other employment statistics—typically come out around 5:30 a.m. Pacific time. These are things that influence economic growth and inflation going forward, which in turn affects bond prices.

For a portfolio manager, eliminating the noise is critical. You have to cut the information flow to a minimum level. You could spend your whole day reading different opinions. For me, that means I don't answer or look at any e-mails I don't want to. Other than for my wife, I'll only pick up the phone three or four times a day. I don't have a cellphone, I don't have a BlackBerry. My motto is "I don't want to be connected—I want to be disconnected." I sit in the middle of a 70-person trading room on the third floor of an office building that overlooks the Pacific Ocean. I'm surrounded by six Bloomberg screens. After I've assimilated the economic releases and market moves, then I've got portfolios to manage. Pimco manages about $550 billion, and I have direct responsibility for about

$200 billion. I check out the status of the various portfolios I manage and determine whether they have enough of this or too much of that, and go to work.

Of course, there some days when there's not much actual trading. When you're managing $200 billion, we need the rest of the market to be accommodating in terms of volume. On a day when there's not much partying going on, it sort of inhibits the ability to get something done. So if you were a fly on the wall, you'd see me just sitting here, examining screens, examining relationships between different bonds or currencies. There's a lot of dull downtime. An outside observer might wonder, "What the hell is he doing to earn that much money?" But that's the nature of the business.

The most important part of my day isn't on the trading floor. Every day at 8:30 a.m., I get up from my desk and walk to a health club across the street. I do yoga and work out for probably an hour and a half, between 8:30 and 10. There's only been two or three times in the past 30 years when someone has come across the street and told me I should get back to the office. One of them was the 1987 market crash. There's an understanding here that that's my haven. Some of my best ideas literally come from standing on my head doing yoga. I'm away from the office, away from the noise, away from the Bloomberg screens—not to mention that standing on your head increases the blood flow to your brain. After about 45 minutes of riding the exercise bike and maybe ten or 15 minutes of yoga, all of a sudden some significant light bulbs seem to turn on. I look at that hour and a half as the most valuable time of the day. —*INTERVIEWED BY JON BIRGER*

Wynton Marsalis,
Artistic Director, Jazz at Lincoln Center

Challenge each other—but don't hold grudges.

You don't want trumpet players and musicians being your primary business decision-maker. It's not possible for me to do that and write music, program the season, and conduct the band. I really do let people do their jobs, so when we come together, we know what each is supposed to do. But I weigh in on everything.

I've never sent an e-mail. I have a computer but haven't plugged it in. I do have a cellphone. I just learned how to text on it. I do everything longhand or talk it out with my staff, and then they type it.

I have to do a lot of other work besides playing and composing—like speeches and fundraising—but everything is for jazz. Even if I'm talking about American culture or American people, it's really about jazz. So it all goes to what my skill set is. I'm really not an organized person. For me, my philosophy is "Just do it all, all the time." I rely on my team. Right now we're writing a script about Count Basie's music for a young people's concert. Phil Schaap, the curator, is responsible for the history element. I explain the music—riffs, breaks, calls and responses, orchestration, short chords—those things I've taught many times. We all talk it together, get an outline, and then revise from that.

In terms of managing the Lincoln Center orchestra, we're part of that continuum of jazz. Our thing is to create the sort of relaxed environment that's part of our music. Most of us came from jazz people, so we have that in us naturally. There are always tensions that come up. Part of working is dealing with tensions. If there's no tension, then you're not serious about what you're doing.

But there's a certain warmth in there, too, and a familiarity. We challenge each other, we fight, but we don't have a lot of grudges. The music is about improvising and being able to create new things at the spur of the moment with other people. There's not a long line of people who can do

> ## "TO FIND A GROOVE
> MEANS PRACTICE, PRACTICE, AND MORE PRACTICE."
> —WYNTON MARSALIS, *Jazz trumpeter*

that in the context of a groove. To find a groove means practice, practice, and more practice. I'm very serious about this. We rehearse a lot, and everybody comes to rehearsal. And I will send you home if you're not playing right.

Now, I do lose my temper. If the young band members aren't practicing, aren't playing right, I will cuss them out. But I'm not volatile. We have the same system of understanding, the music, and a love between each other. It's a flow.

—*INTERVIEWED BY ELLEN MCGIRT*

A.G. Lafley Chairman,
President, and CEO, Procter & Gamble

Take a break, even if you work Sunday nights.

I've learned how to manage my energy. I used to just focus on managing my time. I'd be up in the morning between 5 and 5:30. I'd work out and be at my desk by 6:30 or 7, drive hard until about 7 p.m., then go home, take a break with my wife, Margaret, and be back at it later that evening. I was just grinding through the day.

During my first year in this job, I worked every Saturday and every Sunday morning. Now I work really hard for an hour or an hour and a half. Then I take a break. I walk around and chitchat with people. It can take five or 15 minutes to recharge. It's kind of like the interval training that an athlete does.

I learned this in a program called the Corporate Athlete that we put on for P&G managers. I did the two-day program, where I also learned to change the way I eat. I used to eat virtually nothing for breakfast. Now I have a V-8 juice, half a bagel, and a cup of yogurt. And I eat five or six times a day. It's about managing your glycemic level. You don't want to boom and bust.

The other piece of the Corporate Athlete program is spiritual—things you can do to calm the mind. I've tried to teach myself to meditate. When I travel, which is 60 percent of the time, I find that meditating for five, ten, or 15 minutes in a

> ## "I FIND THAT MEDITATION IN A HOTEL ROOM CAN BE AS GOOD AS A WORKOUT."
> —A.G. LAFLEY, *Procter & Gamble*

hotel room at night can be as good as a workout. Generally, I think I know myself so much better than I used to. And that has helped me stay calm and cool under fire.

A key to staying calm is minimizing the information onslaught. I can't remember the last time I wrote a memo. I write little handwritten notes on my AGL paper, and I send notes, a paragraph or less, on my BlackBerry. I prefer conversations. That's one reason my office and our entire executive floor is open. The CEO office is not typically a warm and welcoming place, but people feel they can come in and talk in mine. We have goofy-looking pink and chartreuse chairs with chrome frames and upholstered backs and seats.

I still work weekends, though not the killer hours I used to. On Sunday nights, [HR chief] Dick Antoine and I get together at his house or my house or on the phone and go through some part of our leadership development program. We started doing this shortly after I became CEO, because I know that the single biggest contribution I will make to this company is helping the next generation of leaders become the best that they can be. —*INTERVIEWED BY PATRICIA SELLERS*

Amy Schulman,
Partner, DLA Piper Rudnick Gray Cary

Be compulsively organized—and delegate.

Many successful women have become successful because they're just awfully good at being compulsive and organized and doers. But at some point, that becomes paralyzing. I think men have traditionally been much better at not micromanaging. It's hard to be successful and be a control freak, because if you cling to things, you're going to be a bottleneck. Delegating to other people—appropriately delegating—is very liberating. There isn't anybody on my team I don't trust 100 percent. Remember, I've been building this team for ten years.

I have two assistants now. I have an assistant from 7 in the morning till 4 in the afternoon, and then an assistant from 4 to midnight. I wake up somewhere between 5 and 6 a.m., and get to the office about 8, before the phone calls start. On the days that I'm not traveling—I travel probably 50 percent of my life—I try to get home by 7:30 p.m. I typically don't sign off e-mail until midnight.

I get around 600 e-mails a day. I divide them into four categories, and I deal with them immediately, by and large. First are e-mails that I forward to someone else. Next are where somebody's giving me information that I need to cascade to somebody else with instructions. Third are the ones that I can read later on an airplane. Fourth are those that require me to respond immediately.

I used to have two cellphones because coverage is erratic. I decided one service provider worked best here and the other there. At some point I decided that was insane.

I don't leave my cellphone on. I'm often in meetings or with clients, and I don't want people to assume that they can dial my cellphone and get me, unless it's an emergency. You can't leave it on if you're in a meeting with the CEO or a witness. It's really important to focus on the problem at hand. You get into a rhythm of a conversation, and you have to honor that rhythm. People get anxious when they feel they're going to be interrupted. What a good lawyer brings to a problem, in addition to creative solutions, is a quality of attentiveness. You can't listen with half an ear.

The BlackBerry was at first a significant intrusion on family life. But my family has gotten used to the fact that I'm more relaxed if I can take care of my e-mails. I don't generally look at my e-mail during mealtimes, and I try not to look at it in movie theaters.

Everybody I know who has a BlackBerry has a good BlackBerry-falling-down-the-toilet story. Mine did while I was flying across country. There was one of those NO FOREIGN OBJECTS signs, and I thought, "Oh, my God, there goes the fuselage." So I run out and I say to the flight attendant, "I'm really sorry, my BlackBerry's fallen down there."And I guess this had happened to her so many times, she said, "Well, do you want some gloves and, like, you can reach in?" I like my BlackBerry, but there's absolutely no way I'm sticking my hand down an airplane toilet to get it. I thought, "God, there are people who have actually taken gloves and done this?" — *INTERVIEWED BY ROGER PARLOFF*

Vera Wang,
CEO, Vera Wang Group

Get away from the routine.

My bedroom is my sanctuary. It's like a refuge, and it's where I do a fair amount of designing—at least conceptually, if not literally. I spread out on my side of the bed, and I may be looking at books to get ideas, or just thinking things through. Staffers send me stuff at home, and I always read it at night—the only time when seven people aren't coming to me at once. I'm able to think in a more peaceful way than when I'm in my normal routine. My normal routine is pretty much putting out fires all day in my office.

It's hard to juggle being a businessperson with being a creative person. You have to organize yourself—PR needs me for PR, and the licensing division needs me for licensing, the bridal people need me for bridal. I prioritize by going to the next collection that's due. And as the collections get bigger, it gets more challenging.

I hate phones. All businesses are personal businesses, and I always try my best to get back to people, but sometimes the barrage of calls is so enormous that if I just answered calls, I would do nothing else. I ask my assistant, P.J., to find out if someone needs an answer in three minutes—or can they wait two days, or can we make a date for when I get back to them? Now, if I were to go near e-mail, there would be even more obligations, and I would be in Bellevue with a white jacket on.

My staff is always able to reach me. As an owner I am always accessible. That's the big difference. I am the CEO, not the COO, but at times I've still had to be partial COO to fix all the myriad things that can go wrong: calm dissatisfied clients, handle employees who want to leave, or renegotiate. These things are very hard to manage in addition to being creative. And that is the challenge of owning a creative business.—
INTERVIEWED BY JIA LYNN YANG

John McCain,
U.S. Senator (R-Arizona)

It's a game of pinball, and you're the ball.

The hardest thing to do is to establish priorities. This morning we had a committee meeting on telecommunications. Now, I'm for à la carte cable. I don't see why some widow from Sun City should have to pay for ESPN if she doesn't want to. At the same time, I had to bounce over to the Armed Services Committee—we're involved with what I think is a scandal with a C-130 cargo airplane. Then I just met with Chamber of Commerce President Tom Donahue, who worked with me on immigration. Later I'm going to meet with a group of people on lobbying reform. And then I'll be meeting with a Congressman who wants me to help him out on something. The key is deciding what are the most important issues to focus on. Priorities come from the constituents, and a lot of it is instinct by now. I've been in this business a long time.

I read my e-mails, but I don't write any. I'm a

Neanderthal—I don't even type. I do have rudimentary capabilities to call up some websites, like *The New York Times* online, that sort of stuff. No laptop. No PalmPilot. I prefer my schedule on note cards, which I keep in my jacket pocket. But my wife has enormous capability. Whenever I want something, I ask her to do it. She's just a wizard. She even does my boarding passes-people can do that now. When we go to the movies,

---

"I DON'T WRITE E-MAILS. I'M A NEANDERTHAL— I DON'T EVEN TYPE."
—JOHN McCAIN, *Republican Senator from Arizona*

---

she gets the tickets ahead of time. It's incredible.

My most valuable resource is my chief of staff and writing partner, Mark Salter. We've been together for 17 years. I cannot imagine my professional life without him. When we're writing a book or speech, he'll come in to the office in the afternoon or evening with a tape recorder. We talk about the outline, then the details of it, then get into the minutiae. He writes most of it, and then we go over it together.

It's the perfect partnership, with him doing most of the work. He's a remarkable man. I gave a speech on the floor of the Senate to wrap up the debate on the torture amendment. It was the only time when there was total silence on the floor of the Senate. We wrote that together.

I rely on staff to take care of things that I know they can, usually back in Arizona. We've got very talented, experienced people who take care of constituent issues. People don't care if I personally get involved, or if I put somebody who is a hell of a lot smarter than I am on it. But if something is important for me to pay attention to, like immigration issues, which have grown for us since 9/11—I focus on it.

We decide on a case-by-case basis about whether to do the

Sunday shows, if it would have some value to get my viewpoint or knowledge out there. I'm going to do Jon Stewart again, and *The Colbert Report*. That's good stuff, an interesting audience for me.

You lose battles in politics. I do get good and angry. Really angry! By God, I'm not going to let them beat me again. I don't like to lose. After the 2000 race for the presidential nomination, I spent at least ten days—and in many ways it was the most wonderful experience of my life—wallowing in self-pity. It was really fun. Freeing. Then I just woke up and said it was time to get over this. The people you represent don't want you this way. You're still their Senator. And besides, America doesn't like sore losers. I also don't hold grudges. It's a waste of time. What's the point? Frankly, the sweetest revenge is success. —*INTERVIEWED BY ELLEN McGIRT*

Jane Friedman,
CEO, HarperCollins

Be open to ideas that come over the transom.

Really, I have to admit: I'm an e-mail addict. It keeps me connected to work even when I'm not at the office. I do about an hour of e-mail in the morning after I've skimmed the newspapers. I usually have to go out for lunch, but I hate it. I'd rather have lunch at my desk and read though e-mails between meetings. My day usually ends in the office at about six o'clock, but then I go to two or three parties a night. Authors, who are the most important people in our company, really appreciate it when the CEO turns up at their event. In between, I check e-mail on my BlackBerry. I can write answers, but I still don't know how to compose e-mails on it. I don't love my BlackBerry, but it keeps me in touch with things. Then, no matter when I get home at night—and it's usually late—I do at least an hour or two of e-mail. It's usually when I'm watching *Law & Order* reruns.

I have this thing about reading all my e-mails. Most people just go delete, delete, delete, but I don't. Other than obvious spam, I read everything that comes in, even unsolicited proposals. I don't read the whole thing, but I'll read the cover letters, and there are moments I feel that somebody has something. I got an e-mail from a 12-year-old Chinese girl that sounded so wonderful to me that I sent it over to the children's division, and they're going to be publishing her book. It's called *Snowbird*.

—*INTERVIEWED BY DEVIN LEONARD*

> "MOST PEOPLE JUST GO DELETE, DELETE, DELETE. I READ EVERYTHING."
> —JANE FRIEDMAN, *HarperCollins CEO*

Judge Richard Posner,
U.S. Court of Appeals for the Seventh Circuit, Chicago

Seek the most efficient mode of communication.

I usually think of the digital revolution in terms of reducing the costs of transferring information. For people like me, whose work is basically intellectual and not heavily dependent on personal contacts, the effect is wholly positive. The older, conventional means of collecting, communicating, and manipulating information were very inferior. It's also enabled me to work at home.

I came here from lunch with a political theorist at NYU, and it was an extremely valuable conversation. For him to convey his comments about my book, a conversation was the most efficient mode of communication. It's just that in my line of work, that type of face-to-face or even voice-to-voice communication is relatively infrequent. I have very, very few telephone conversations.

I have become entirely e-mail dependent in the sense that

I would not dream of going anywhere overnight without my laptop. I can't even substitute a BlackBerry because so much of the stuff that I get involves substantial attachments. So I carry a laptop everywhere. With e-mail there's a kind of oppression factor, especially on Mondays. But it's a very small price to pay.

I usually get up around a quarter to 8 and don't get to the office till about 9:30, 10 a.m. I usually go home after lunch and then spend the rest of the afternoon and evening, except for dinner, up till about 11:30 p.m., working. I'm working on opinions, or writing a book or blog, or something else.

When court is in session, we hear six cases a day, sitting in three-judge panels, and split it up so that each judge does two opinions. I usually write my first draft of the two opinions in the evening after the arguments. So maybe four hours' worth of time to write two opinions. I'm a very fast writer. I can write 20, 30 manuscript pages in an evening. I do revisions later, but I find it more efficient to get something down that indicates where the gaps in my thinking are, and what research has to be done, and so on. —*INTERVIEWED BY ROGER PARLOFF*

Hank Paulson,
Former Chairman and CEO, Goldman Sachs

Work the phone—and the clock.

I've never used e-mail, but I'm a huge voicemail user. I do a couple hundred voicemails a day. And I return every call right away, whether it's a client or someone in the firm. There are positives and negatives to this. I don't have a lot of time for small talk. Occasionally there are wing nuts who call, and I pass them on to Julie, my assistant. But Julie doesn't screen my voicemails. The people at Goldman Sachs have to be able to get to me. Clients have to be able to get to me.

I've always spent a lot of time on the phone. Even when

cellphones were a novelty in the 1980s, when I lived in Chicago, I was using one of those huge Motorola phones as I walked from the train station to the office. This past Christmas, my wife, Wendy, and my daughter, Amanda, and her husband and I spent ten days hiking in Chile, and my daughter took so many pictures of me with this big satellite phone attached to my ear.

When I got back to the office in January, I called 60 CEOs in the first week to wish them happy New Year. I had never done that before, but it was great. I asked them about their business and their relationship with Goldman. I spend at least a third of my time on Goldman people and culture—we have to be the employer of choice in our industry. So I spend time at business schools and am very involved in recruiting. In 2005 we started a Chairman's Forum to raise awareness of the importance of business judgment. I taught more than 25 sessions to all 1,200 of our managing directors in Asia, Europe, and the U.S. That's culture-building.

Forty percent of our earnings comes from outside the U.S., so I travel a lot. Whenever I travel, I take time to exercise. When I go to China—which I've been to about 70 times in the past 16 years—I book my flight so it arrives at 6 a.m., which is the earliest you can land. I check into the hotel and go right to the treadmill in the gym. Then, starting at 8 a.m., I'll go back to back to back until 9 at night. I'll get up the next day and do the same thing. I make sure to leave in the evening so I can be back at work in my office in New York the next morning.

I've always been very efficient and disciplined. If I have a business dinner, people know that it should start at 6:30 and be over by 8:30. When I'm home in New York, I'm asleep at 10. I'm up at 5:30 and try to work out four or five times a week. Once or twice a week, I run four miles in Central Park. I used to do seven-minute miles. Now I'm up to eight-and-a-half or nine. —*INTERVIEWED BY PATRICIA SELLERS*

Great
DECISIONS

*Making the Right
Choice at the Right Time*

GREAT DECISIONS

Making the Right Choice at the Right Time

Picture a hallway. You're walking down it, alone. Before you reach the end, you need to reach a decision. Your engineers have been hard at work on a daring new product. But now the stakes have grown so big that ... well, you wouldn't be betting just the farm at this point. You'd be betting the farm, the house, and the kids. And your rival—a far more established firm—has upped the ante, promising a product that has sent your engineers back to the drawing board. Now you're about to meet with your biggest potential customer. And you have two choices: You can make a bet that—if it doesn't bankrupt your company outright—might repay itself sometime in the next couple of decades. Or you can keep your chips safe for another day.

What do you do? If your instincts say, "Walk away," you've made a sound decision—one that would probably pass any discounted-cash-flow test with flying colors. You've also just killed the 707: The plane that vaulted Boeing past Douglas Aircraft.

The man on the spot that day in 1955, Boeing president Bill Allen, wasn't armed with hindsight. What he did have was an iron stomach. In promising American Airlines the jetliner it wanted instead of the one Boeing had geared up to make, Allen took a giant gulp of uncertainty. When the 707 took to the skies three years later, it flew America into the jet age.

But that's the language of history, where everything sounds inevitable. It's a reminder that things now past were once in the future; real people and their choices were the bridge. The best decision-makers were capable of seeing the present as if it were already the past.

So blindfold yourself and imagine you are back in 1876, when the long-distance business involved Morse code, or in 1964, trying to invent a computer age that doesn't yet exist. You don't have a crystal ball to consult. You have a decision to make. —*JERRY USEEM*

DECISIONS THAT MADE HISTORY

*By Jerry Useem; Kate Bonamici; Nelson D. Schwartz;
Cait Murphy; Brent Schlender; Corey Hajim; Ellen Florian Kratz;
Stephanie N. Mehta; Barney Gimbel*

1876: WESTERN UNION HANGS UP ON BELL'S NEW INVENTION

In 1876 a man named Gardiner Hubbard presented the Western Union telegraph company with the chance to buy a set of patents. The asking price? $100,000. The product in question? Alexander Graham Bell's telephone.

Bell had won a technological victory earlier that year, beating another inventor, Elisha Gray, to the patent office by hours. But the all-out effort had left him broke. And his soon-to-be father-in-law, Hubbard, had struggled to convince people that the telephone would be anything more than a parlor trick. So when the newlywed Bells left for an extended honeymoon in Europe, George Sanders (the biggest investor in the enterprise) and Hubbard decided to unload the patents. Western Union was an obvious buyer—it dominated the young business of long-distance communication, controlling the network of telegraph lines crisscrossing the country.

Western Union president William Orton responded, "This 'telephone' has too many shortcomings to be seriously considered as a means of communication. The device is inherently of no value to us." He rejected the offer.

Orton had clashed with Hubbard several years before during an attempt to break Western Union's monopoly on telegraph lines. Not only was he uninterested in providing Hubbard with financial gain, but Orton had faith that, should the telephone amount to anything, his giant corporation would be able to force Bell out of the market without trouble.

It didn't take long for Western Union to recognize the magnitude of its blunder. Within the year Western Union began hearing that its customers were replacing teletypes with phones leased from the newly founded Bell Co. So the company hastily put out its own version of the telephone, using Elisha Gray's patents and a design by Thomas Edison. A furious legal battle followed. Tiny Bell Co. prevailed—and Western Union was forced to lease telephone equipment from Bell.

Though it would take Bell Co. several years to get on solid financial footing, the baton had been passed: Western Union began to decline. Bell and its successor, AT&T, would rule the communications industry for the next century. —KATE BONAMICI

1903: KING GILLETTE DECIDES TO THROW AWAY THE BLADES

Today America is awash in disposable diapers, disposable cameras, even disposable clothes. But when a former bottle-cap salesman from Boston named King Camp Gillette started selling safety razors with disposable blades in 1903, people weren't disposed to throw things away. The very idea of discarding something without reusing or repairing it ran counter to American notions of thrift. But Gillette, a part-time inventor whose earlier patents included an improved beer tap, had taken the advice of his boss at Crown Cork & Seal, William Painter, inventor of the bottle cap. "Think of something which, once used, is thrown away," Painter told him, "and the customer keeps coming back for more."

Gillette was staring at his dull razor one morning when that thing came to him. Like other razors of the day, his blade required time-consuming "stropping" and professional resharpenings to remain useful. Gillette spent the next eight years figuring out how to cast a blade thin enough—and therefore cheap enough-to throw away when it got dull. In 1901 he patented the first razor with a disposable blade.

Persuading men to buy it was easier than convincing them they could dispose of it. As Russell Adams relates in *King Gillette: The Man and His Wonderful Shaving Device*, Sinclair Lewis's fictional salesman, Babbitt, tossed his used blades atop a medicine cabinet "with a mental note" to do something about the pile. H.L. Mencken claimed he put his in the church collection plate. Some barbers offered illicit resharpening services. King Gillette offered this proposal: Drop your used blades off to be resharpened; then never pick them up.

Contrary to myth, Gillette never did "give away the razor and sell the blade." The kit cost a hefty $5. But the U.S. Army gave 3.5 million Gillette razors and 32 million blades to soldiers during World War I, hooking a generation—and planting the beginnings of America's throwaway culture. —*KATE BONAMICI*

1906: GIANNINI OPENS HIS VAULTS AFTER THE QUAKE

A.P. Giannini had one thing on his mind when he was bounced out of bed by the great San Francisco earthquake: his bank. Rushing into the shattered city, he managed to load $80,000 in gold—removed from the deposit vaults of his Bank of Italy by two quick-thinking employees—onto a horse cart, covered with vegetables, before fire consumed the building. Other banks' vaults would be too hot to open for weeks. When his fellow bankers proposed a six-month banking moratorium at a meeting the day after, Giannini broke ranks. "In November," he argued, "there will be no city or people left to serve." He was open for business the next day at a makeshift desk in North Beach, offering to lend money "on a face and a name."

The gesture made Giannini's own name. And it reflected his democratic philosophy: The money in the vaults wasn't there to serve banks. It was there to serve customers. The son of Italian immigrants, Giannini had founded the Bank of Italy in 1904 on the premise that banks should serve more than the fortunate few. Offering loans of $10 to $300 to anyone who had a job, Giannini also convinced those in the working class that they should turn their tin cans of savings over to a bank.

It was Giannini who popularized home mortgages, auto loans, and other pioneering forms of consumer credit. As he expanded his reach by opening branch offices—another new idea—throughout California, he backed unproven businesses like Hollywood (loaning Walt Disney $2 million for *Snow White*) and the California wine industry. By 1945 his legacy was just about everywhere. His renamed Bank of America was the largest bank in the world. Access to credit had become a cornerstone of middle-classdom. And a few years after his death in 1949, BofA would introduce the public to another new concept: the credit card. —*Kate Bonamici*

1914: Ford offers $5 a day

The first of them arrived at 3 a.m. By daybreak some 4,000 were huddled in the deep January freeze. By 7:30, 10,000 men had gathered at the entrance to the Highland Park, Mich., factory, hoping for a job at a wage that sounded too good to be true.

But it was true. The previous morning, Henry Ford had lingered near a window while his treasurer read a statement to reporters: "At one stroke, [Ford] will reduce the hours of labor from nine to eight" and offer its workers "five dollars per day"—more than twice the prevailing wage of $2.34.

The 1914 announcement hit America like a thunderclap. *The Wall Street Journal* accused Ford of "an economic blunder if not crimes." But Ford's motives were neither socialist nor utopian. Ever since his assembly lines had lurched into motion the year before, he simply could not keep workers. Turnover of 370 percent required hiring almost 50,000 people a year just to maintain a workforce of 14,000. Putting $5 in a worker's pocket, Ford hoped, would do more than reward him for grueling and mind-numbing work. It would turn him into a consumer. At one stroke, that is, Ford could mass-produce both a car and a market for it. He could also play social engineer: To qualify for that $5, workers would have to remain in good moral standing (no saloons) and submit to intrusive home visits from Ford's Sociology Department.

In one sense, the $5 day changed nothing. Discontinued in 1917, it was a distant memory by the time Ford goons beat up labor organizers in 1937. But it also changed everything. For the first time, a major industrialist had suggested that the contract between employer and employee consisted of more than just a wage (and the lowest possible one at that). By the 1950s that relationship had deepened to include pensions, dental insurance, and the ultimate symbol of corporate paternalism: the gold watch. —*JERRY USEEM*

1925: SEARS GETS PHYSICAL

In 1940, Sears Roebuck turned out the lights for the last time, disbanding its workforce of 25,000. Just decades earlier, its catalogs had been eagerly awaited in the nation's farm towns and prairies. But its once reliable customers had begun motoring into town—if not to live there, then to shop. Time had passed the company by.

It's a history that might have been. But Sears had a leader who saw history coming and was determined to beat it to the punch.

Gen. Robert F. Wood, business historian Richard Tedlow writes in his new book, *New and Improved*, "was one of those fortunate few to whom numbers spoke." As an Army logistics officer coordinating construction of the Panama Canal, Wood developed an "odd passion" for The Statistical Abstract of the United States. Upon his return from World War I, the numbers were telling an important story. Farm income was dropping. Automobile registrations were rising. And the so-called chain stores of James C. Penney were multiplying.

Wood spelled it out for his new employer, Sears' archrival, Montgomery Ward, in a 1921 memorandum. "[W]e can beat the chain stores at their own game," he wrote. "We have four distribution points; we have an organized purchasing system; we have a wonderful name if we choose to take advantage of it." Management blocked the idea—then fired Wood in 1924. He went straight to Sears, was named president within four years, and plunged ahead with his plan.

Imagine today an overnight assault of Amazon.com superstores, and you might begin to grasp the magnitude of this decision. Sears operated out of Chicago, period. Where would it put its new stores? Who would manage them? How do you treat a live customer? Nothing in the company's past had prepared it for those challenges. But its leader had a different past. "Business is like war in one respect," Wood said. "If its grand strategy is correct, any number of tactical errors can be made."

The errors were numerous and costly. The blitz of store openings—more than 300 in just three years—caused Sears to report a loss for only the second time in its history. Bitter feuds erupted between catalog men and store managers. "We had a 100 percent record of mistakes," Wood would say later. And the early stores looked ridiculous: Placed near highways outside cities, they were surrounded by vast parking lots and little else. Eventually, though, the cities engulfed them, and suburbanites filled the parking lots. By 1931 store sales surpassed catalog revenue. And in 1934, Sears opened a peculiar-looking store. It had no windows, like a big box. —*JERRY USEEM*

1935: PAN AM FLIES THE OCEAN BLUE

The record of business in the 1930s is a somber one—bankruptcy, failure, and the loss of those animal spirits that are as important to capitalism as capital. There are a few exceptions.

Hollywood is making great flicks; the Twinkie is invented—and aviation takes off. In the wake of Charles Lindbergh's solo flight across the Atlantic in 1927, aviation grew briskly, but leaving the country still meant taking a boat. Juan Trippe, the founder of Pan American World Airways, would change that. The patrician son of a New York investment banker (belying his first name, he had no Hispanic roots), Trippe had been rudely shut out of the lucrative U.S. airmail business. So he decided to become king of the international airways instead.

He started flying to Latin America, a sensible choice since the region required only short hops over water and his planes could find landing spots all along the way. At first Pan Am was strictly a mail service. Then Trippe realized that a passenger or two would boost profits, so he installed a couple of wicker seats. "Fly with us to Havana," went one ad, "and you can bathe in Bacardi rum four hours from now."

And then, in a decision that must have seemed like madness at the time, he set his sights slightly farther away—China. This raised a few problems: big oceans, limited range, primitive navigation, and lack of runways. And it was not at all clear that there was a market for flights to Asia. But Trippe was so sure that the world would eventually catch up to his own expansive views of aviation that he did it anyway. In November 1935, Pan Am inaugurated transpacific airmail service with the China Clipper. These flying boats could take off and land on water; they hopped to Hong Kong in about a week via stops in Hawaii, Wake, Midway, Guam, and the Philippines. The first passenger service came a year later. The cost was steep, about $11,000 one way in today's dollars, but cattle class this wasn't. Late-model Clippers featured sleeping berths, a separate dining area, a VIP lounge, and dressing rooms.

In 1939, Pan Am began the first transatlantic service, the Yankee Clipper. Passengers flew in a luxuriously appointed Boeing 314 double-decker, which even had a honeymoon suite. The 29-hour flights were too expensive for the middle class, but they helped build the idea that flying was not just for daredevils and the mail anymore. Between 1935 and 1940 the number of Americans making international flights soared.

Trippe's decision to launch the China Clipper and then the Yankee Clipper provided the fuel for the takeoff of mass international aviation. He has a lot to answer for. —*CAIT MURPHY*

1950: DEMING CHARTS JAPAN'S REMARKABLE COURSE

Sometimes big decisions are made to the blare of banner headlines. And sometimes they are made quietly, with no more drama than a puff of air. At a dinner party in Tokyo in the summer of 1950, 21 of Japan's most influential corporate leaders, who accounted for some 80 percent of the country's industrial capacity, made the latter kind of decision. What they did was listen—specifically to W. Edwards Deming, an obscure American statistician who had never met a payroll and had been to Japan only once before. Deming was nonetheless certain that he knew how to solve postwar Japan's economic problems. "You can send quality out and get food back," he told his skeptical audience.

The pursuit of quality, Deming said, was the key to higher productivity, bigger profits, more jobs, and therefore a richer society. Quality, he lectured, did not begin by finding defects at the end of the production line. It had to be pursued along every link of the supply chain, with the active cooperation of everyone from suppliers to the humblest worker on the factory floor. If Japanese companies followed his 14 points, Deming promised his dinner companions and other managers in a series of lectures that summer, their goods would be world-class in five years. The notion seemed ridiculous. At the time, the term "Made in Japan" was such a joke that some factory owners set up operations in the village of Usa so that they could mark their products "Made in USA." But Japan's poohbahs didn't have any better ideas, so they decided to take up Deming's challenge.

In 1957, Toyota exported its first car to the U.S.—a clunker, as it happens. But by the 1980s, Japan looked ready to eat everyone's economic lunch. Deming's sardonic comment: "Don't blame the Japanese. We did it to ourselves." (And don't blame Deming for Japan's current economic problems, which have to do with banking and politics, not quality.)

Indeed, Deming was the classic prophet without honor in his own country. It wasn't until the '80s that U.S. manufacturers adopted his principles—largely to meet the competition from Japan. Deming's 14 points are now standard operating procedure around the world. —*CAIT MURPHY*

1964: THOMAS WATSON JR. DOES A 360

So you've just bought a new computer. Very exciting. Only thing is, the files on your old computer are useless. You need to rewrite all your programs. And your printer won't work anymore. Nothing is compatible! But then, that's how things went before IBM's System/360.

IBM's "$5,000,000,000 Gamble," as *Fortune* called it in 1966, grew out of the company's own compatibility problems. Rivalry between the company's two divisions produced a "wildly disorganized" array of offerings, CEO Thomas J. Watson Jr. recalled in his autobiography, *Father, Son & Co.* It was T. Vincent Learson, one of the "harsh, scratchy types" Watson valued (and who would eventually succeed him as CEO), who gathered executives from across the company at the New Englander Motor Hotel near Stamford, Conn. Two weeks before Christmas 1961, he essentially locked the doors and told them they couldn't come out until they had reached some conclusions.

On Dec. 28 the group delivered an 80-page report to Watson. It was the birth certificate of the System/360, a family of computers that would remain compatible with future generations-and would render all previous computers, including those of IBM itself, obsolete. As *Fortune* put it, "It was roughly as though General Motors had decided to scrap its existing makes and models and offer in their place one new line of cars, covering the entire spectrum of demand, with a radically redesigned engine and an exotic fuel."

As if that weren't challenge enough, Watson promised to roll out the new line-consisting of six computers and 44 peripherals—all at once rather than piecemeal, to make a "tremendous splash." It turned out to be a tremendous stretch, requiring four years, 65,000 additional employees, and five new factories. But a flood of orders, while nearly capsizing IBM, established a new standard. For the first time the world's computers had a common language. Every time you painlessly upgrade your own desktop, you can think of the project that brought IBM to the brink. —COREY HAJIM

1970: CURT FLOOD REFUSES TO PLAY BALL

"I have only two choices," a seething Curt Flood told his wife, Marian, in late 1969. "I can go to Philadelphia, or I can quit baseball altogether. I will not go to Philadelphia."

No one quite believed that Flood, star center fielder on three World Series teams in St. Louis, would pass up the princely salary of $90,000 for a principle. But Flood wasn't merely unhappy over his trade to a city considered unfriendly to blacks. His main objection was baseball's "reserve clause," the century-old system that allowed owners to hoard and swap players as a kid trades baseball cards but banned the players from shopping their own talents. Flood wrote in his 1971 book, *The Way It Is*: "A salesman reluctant to transfer from one office to another may choose to seek employment on the sales force of a different firm. A plumber can reject the dictates of his boss without relinquishing his right to plumb elsewhere ... But [if the athlete] elects not to work for the corporation that 'owns' his services, baseball forbids him to ply his trade at all. In the hierarchy of living things, he ranks with poultry."

This was more than unfair, Flood argued. It was un-American. On Christmas Eve, Flood put his stance in writing: "I believe I have the right to consider offers from other clubs," he wrote baseball commissioner Bowie Kuhn, and "request that you ... advise them of my availability for the 1970 season."

Kuhn refused. Flood sued and lost. In 1975, though, pitchers Dave McNally and Andy Messersmith challenged the reserve clause—and won. Free agency was born. It would transform the sports business, while typifying a new, larger shift from lifetime employment to worker mobility. Today's multimillionaire ballplayers made out well. But Flood's decision cost him. He sat out all of 1970, and played just 13 games with the lowly Washington Senators in 1971 before retiring, at age 31. He died in 1997. —*JERRY USEEM*

1972: FORD DECIDES TO LET THE PINTO EXPLODE

In the early 1970s, Dennis Gioia, a newly hired recall coordinator at Ford, heard scattered tales that the company's popular new compact, the Pinto, "lit up" when hit in a rear-end collision. But it was only after seeing a crumpled Pinto in Ford's "Chamber of Horrors," where damaged cars were examined for possible flaws, that he wondered whether there was a serious problem. "My revulsion on seeing this incinerated hulk was immediate and profound," he wrote in a 1992 article for the *Journal of Business Ethics*.

Gioia brought the problem before the recall committee, but, lacking evidence of a systemic problem, joined them in voting against a recall. About a year later they got some evidence. During preproduction crash tests, they learned, eight of 11 Pintos had "suffered potentially catastrophic gas tank ruptures" on impact. The fuel tanks of the three other cars had survived only because they'd been shielded from a set of studs that did the puncturing.

For the second time the committee voted, and for a second time it decided not to act. The logic was clear: Conventional wisdom held that small cars were inherently unsafe, and as Ford president Lee Iacocca put it, safety didn't sell. Fixing the problem would probably reduce storage space, already at a premium, and ultimately, the design was legal.

The issue arose a third time in 1977, but now in the pages of *Mother Jones* magazine. Writer Mark Dowie had acquired a Ford cost-benefit analysis from the early '70s that compared the cost of recalling all Ford cars with rear-mounted fuel tanks (not just Pintos) against the costs of restitution for the families of those injured or killed by the Pinto's flaw. It would be cheaper, by a factor of three to one, to pay off victims and their families than to make an $11 fix in each car.

A public still reeling from the betrayal of Watergate now learned that one of its great corporations, Ford Motor Co., had weighed the lives of consumers against the dollar—and chosen the dollar. Ford discontinued the Pinto in 1980 after a costly recall, but the blow to trust would prove more lasting. Consumer activists would now act as safety watchdogs. And when a California jury awarded a Pinto victim a then unheard-of $125 million (later reduced to $3.5 million) for pain and suffering, it galvanized class-action lawyers everywhere. —*KATE BONAMICI*

1975: WALTER WRISTON AUTOMATES THE TELLER

John Reed was operating on faith. He knew he was right, though he didn't know why. Fortunately Reed's boss, Citibank chairman Walter Wriston, was also a believer in the possibilities that technology could bring to banking. So in 1975, Wriston agreed to sink an eye-popping $100 million into Reed's plan. Two years later the bank went public with it. Then, virtually overnight, Citi dotted the Big Apple with a network of more than 400 automatic teller machines, according to Phillip Zweig's biography, *Wriston*.

No one knew if bank customers would forgo dealing with a live teller. But Wriston was impatient to get Citibank's consumer business growing. "The demand deposits in the city of New York had not grown in ten years," Wriston told *Fortune* in an interview in 2005, before his death from cancer. "It was perfectly clear that something had to be done."

The gamble paid off—with a little help from above. In early 1978, New York City was walloped with more than a foot of snow. Within three days a commercial ran showing New Yorkers trekking through the slush to Citibank ATMs. A catchphrase was born: "The Citi Never Sleeps." Use of the machines soared. By 1981, Citi's share of New York deposits had doubled. Rivals stopped snickering about Citi's "soulless machines" and started to get with the program. Today, of course, getting money in Paris from your bank account in Portland seems as mundane as traffic lights. "But when you think about it," said Wriston, "it's just extraordinary." Machines, everywhere, that give you money. —*ELLEN FLORIAN KRATZ*

1980: REG JONES PICKS JACK

Before his name became synonymous with General Electric, Jack Welch was the anti-GE. He railed at its bureaucracy, ran his Pittsfield, Mass., division as if it were Jack Welch Plastics, and heaped scorn on the "dinks" who ruled at headquarters. In their urbane world, Welch was odd man out.

Yet it was one of their number—the courtly Reginald Jones—who made Welch odd man in, naming him CEO in 1980. The consequences of Jones's decision are well known. By tearing up GE in the absence of any outward crisis, Welch became a pariah—and then, as global competition tore up one U.S. company after another, an icon whose street-fighting instincts inspired book titles like *Business the Jack Welch Way*, *Jack Welch Speaks*, and *Jack Welch and the G.E. Way*.

Welch's name had actually been excluded from an early list of successor candidates. He was too young, too impatient, too reckless. He stammered. But in 1979, Jones closed the door to his office, drew on his pipe, and said to Welch, "You and I are flying in one of the company's planes, and this plane crashes. Who should be chairman?" Like many of the six other finalists, Welch first tried to climb out of the wreckage. But over the next two hours Welch delivered a critique of GE that resonated with Jones.

Like Welch, Jones saw danger on the horizon. As a director at Bethlehem Steel, he'd seen what happens when foreign competition hits a slumbering bureaucracy, and he feared what it might do to GE. "The first thing you do when you're looking for a successor is, don't look for someone like you," Jones told a Harvard Business School class in 1982. "The other thing is, you'd better look to the environment ahead ... [and] get someone who's gonna be attuned to that environment, not the environment in which you lived." Jones's last and perhaps best decision at GE was to pick a decision-maker who would change the way GE made decisions. —*JERRY USEEM*

1983: SAM WALTON EXPLORES THE FINAL FRONTIER

Wal-Mart's founder was not a technophile. He was a grounded man, and a cheap one. But in 1983, when his subordinates proposed a $24 million investment involving outer space, he listened.

It was Glenn Habern, a data-processing manager, who came up with the idea of building a private satellite network. It was far-fetched, to be sure: Wal-Mart would be the retail test case for this kind of technology. But it had two selling points. The first was personal contact. Walton was adamant about visiting every store personally. The growing number of stores, though, was making that harder and harder. A satellite system would let him beam pep talks to his associates.

The second selling point was data. Walton couldn't get enough of it, and the company's jammed telephone lines couldn't handle it. Satellites allowed him to check on how inventory was piling up, track a day's sales at a particular store, see whether a new product was sitting on the shelves. "With a company, the risk you run is that you grow so rapidly that it gets out of control, that you can't get your arms around it," said David Glass, Wal-Mart's president at the time (and its CEO from 1988 to 2000). "People started asking, 'How you gonna communicate with all these people when you get larger?' We had a very strong culture, but we worried about that."

Walton "didn't like the technology part" of the pitch, Glass recalls. "He was a merchant first and foremost." But the video broadcasts sealed the deal: "He loved the idea of being able to talk to all the associates." Four years later, when Walton addressed a video camera in an old Wal-Mart warehouse, the broadcast was beamed 22,300 miles skyward and received at roughly 1,000 Wal-Mart stores.

The world's biggest private satellite network gave Wal-Mart a huge informational advantage and the power to combine size with speed. Sales growth, already stunning, hit warp speed. In 1985, two years before the completion of the system, Wal-Mart's sales were $8.4 billion. Ten years later they were $93.6 billion. Ten years after that, they had left the atmosphere altogether: $288 billion, a number without historical precedent. —COREY HAJIM

1984: MA BELL GIVES AWAY HER BABIES

Charlie Brown was on the hot seat. American Telephone & Telegraph, after prospering for nearly a century as the only phone company most of the country had ever known, was under attack for being too powerful. Congress and the Federal

Communications Commission wanted to make it easier for other companies to compete. The Department of Justice was pursuing an antitrust suit that essentially sought to dismantle the company. It was clear to Brown, chairman of AT&T since 1979, that his employees and shareholders couldn't take more uncertainty.

So in 1982, Brown announced the previously unthinkable: AT&T would voluntarily break itself up on Jan. 1, 1984. The company wouldn't forfeit its equipment-making arm, Western Electric, nor would it lose Bell Labs, the storied research facility that invented the vacuum tube, the transistor, and the laser. And it would keep its most profitable business—long distance. Instead Ma Bell would spin off her "babies," the seven local phone companies that provided dial tones to most of the nation.

Brown had been widely expected to do just the opposite, keeping most of the babies while losing Western Electric. But Brown and his lieutenants believed that the worlds of communications and computing were coming together. By owning a combination of long-distance and technology assets—weren't telephone switches just big computers anyway?—AT&T would remain as powerful as ever. And while they knew long distance would be opened to competitors, they didn't doubt AT&T's ability to fend off little gnats like MCI.

It was the decision of a man who had never faced the rude realities of cutthroat price competition. But perhaps Brown's most fundamental error was that he didn't grasp how quickly his customers could leave the trusted AT&T brand just to save a few cents a minute. They could and they did—providing a searing lesson in the fickleness of the American consumer. Long-distance lines, it turns out, are easily replicated; local phone networks are not.

Had Brown (who retired in 1986 and died in 2003) guessed that long distance would become a commodity in less than a decade, perhaps he would have fought harder to hold on to the local phone businesses with their steady cash flows and direct connections to millions of consumers. AT&T then wouldn't have embarked on its futile quest to get back into the local phone business, spending billions on wireless and cable assets and this year suffering the indignity of being taken over by one of its own offspring. —STEPHANIE N. MEHTA

1985: DREXEL BURNHAM WRITES A "HIGHLY CONFIDENT" LETTER

It was late one February night, and Carl Icahn wanted to launch a hostile takeover of Phillips Petroleum. Unfortunately, he was $8 billion short, and almost nobody knew who he was. That could have put a damper on his plans. But a financier named Michael Milken had developed a new way of using junk bonds to raise capital. So Icahn asked Drexel Burnham, the second-tier investment bank where Milken worked, for a letter of commitment.

Impossible, responded the Drexel heavies. They didn't actually have the money the way a bank had money. They could raise it only once Icahn launched his takeover: a chicken-and-egg problem. But as the night wore on, Leon Black, head of the firm's mergers and acquisitions department, finally ventured, "Why don't we say we're 'highly confident' that we can raise [the financing]?"

And so the next morning Drexel drew up a letter saying just that. Icahn would end up ditching the Phillips deal, but the era of the corporate raider had begun.

What that letter meant, in practice, was that with little more than a note from Drexel (usually approved by Milken), any fool could get his hands on a huge sum of money to take over—or at least threaten to take over—a major corporation. As Wall Street firms followed Drexel's lead, executives began to face the very real threat of a Carl Icahn or a T. Boone Pickens seizing their companies and throwing them overboard. In 1986 alone, 3,973 takeovers, mergers, and buyouts were completed in the U.S. at a total cost of $236 billion.

The raiders were finally beaten back with laws and poison pills, and Milken pleaded to charges of securities fraud that sent him to prison for 22 months. But the sense of security in the executive suite never returned. As boards started acting like raiders—dumping CEOs who failed to increase their companies' stock prices—executives took up the rallying cry that had once threatened them: "Shareholder value!" Two words that, for good and ill, would define the decade to come.— BARNEY GIMBEL

2000: JERRY LEVIN DECIDES HE DOESN'T NEED A COLLAR

The chairman of Time Warner loved the deal he struck in January 2000 to merge his company with highflier America Online, then valued at about $160 billion. Jerry Levin had such faith in the combination of traditional and new media assets, in fact, that he decided not to place a collar on the transaction. A collar enables the seller—in this case Time Warner—to revisit the terms of the transaction if the buyer's stock falls below a certain price.

Why did he make that choice? "With a collar, the implication is that you are not really sure and you need this kind of protection," Levin would later tell an audience at Manhattan's 92nd Street Y. "I wanted to make a statement that I believe in it." Unfortunately, Levin's belief that AOL could deliver a glittering new-media future proved colossally wrong.

Time Warner shareholders wish Levin hadn't been such a true believer. Almost as soon as the companies announced their historic deal, the Internet bubble burst and AOL shares plunged 50 percent. Without a collar, Time Warner couldn't renegotiate the deal. Some Time Warner executives urged Levin to use the drastic drop in AOL's stock price as an excuse to cancel the merger altogether, or at least as leverage to rework the terms to give Time Warner shareholders a greater stake in the combined company. But Levin never did.

His passion for hooking up with AOL, even as its stock nosedived and questions about the quality of its advertising revenues surfaced, turned a questionable deal into the crowning folly of the dot-com era. Time Warner shareholders—who once owned 100 percent of a company worth $75 billion— today own 45 percent of a company worth, well, roughly $75 billion. —*STEPHANIE N. MEHTA*

JIM COLLINS ON TOUGH CALLS

By Jerry Useem

When he's not out scaling mountains (he's a world class rock climber), author Jim Collins eats, drinks, and sleeps business. So when *Fortune* senior writer Jerry Useem (a sometime Collins collaborator) asked him to discuss the art of decision-making, he got so into the idea that he pored over 14 years of research and interviews he had amassed in the course of writing his business blockbusters *Built to Last* and *Good to Great*. Then, in a series of conversations, he and Useem explored the intriguing insights he had gleaned from analyzing the processes behind key decisions in business history. For example, lasting excellence in corporations seems to stem less from decisions about strategy than decisions about people, and seeking consensus is not the way to make the tough calls. Here are edited highlights of their talks.

What were the surprises when you reexamined your research through the lens of decision-making?

We tend to think that decisions are very much about "what." But when I look at my research notes and I look at interview transcripts from the executives we've interviewed, one theme that comes through is that their greatest decisions were not "what" but "who." They were people decisions.

Why are people decisions so important?
Fundamentally, the world is uncertain. Decisions are about the future and your place in the future when that future is uncertain. So what is the key thing you can do to prepare for that uncertainty? You can have the right people with you.

Let's take a non-business case and a business case to illustrate the importance of the people piece. In 1978, Jim Logan and his partner, Mugs Stump, became the first people to climb the Emperor Face of Mount Robson in the Canadian Rockies. And to this day, everybody else who's tried the face has either died or failed on the route. When I asked Logan, "Why were you able to do the Emperor Face?" he said, "Because I made the single most important decision: I picked the right partner."

He told me that there was this one place, the "death zone," and once they went above it, they really couldn't retreat. They were going to either summit or die—no going back. They didn't know what they were going to find beyond that point, and they didn't know what the weather was going to be. And so, therefore, what's your greatest hedge against uncertainty? Having people who can adapt to whatever the mountain throws at you.

Give us the business example.
Let's take the story of a company heading into a very uncertain world: Wells Fargo in the late 1970s. Everybody knows the storm of deregulation is going to hit. But nobody knows precisely how it's going to shake out. When is it going to hit? What exact form is it going to take? What impact is it going to have on the banking industry? Dick Cooley, chief executive of Wells Fargo at that time, was very clear with us when we did our research. He said, in essence, I did not know what we were going to have to do to prevail through deregulation, because

it was an uncertain set of contingencies. Too many of them. But I did know that if I spent the 1970s building a team of the most capable executives possible, they would figure out what to do when deregulation hit. He couldn't lay down a plan for what was going to happen, because he didn't know what was going to happen. So his decision was actually a bunch of decisions about getting the people who could deal with whatever deregulation turned out to be.

Okay, but once you have great people in place, you still have to make decisions.
Great decisions begin with really great people and a simple statement: I don't know. The research evidence on that is very clear—that the leaders who ended up setting things in place that produced extraordinary results over time, and a series of great decisions over time, really were very comfortable saying "I don't know" until they knew.

And really, they were just being honest. I mean, which is best? Lying—meaning saying you don't know when you've already made up your mind? Or presuming to know when you don't and therefore lying to yourself? Or speaking the truth? Which is, "I don't yet know, but I know we have to get it right."

How do you say that without looking irresolute? Don't people expect leaders to say, clearly, "Here's where we're headed"?
That's the typical thing that happens in companies. The CEO has already made a decision, and his definition of leadership is to get people to participate so that they feel good about the decision he's already made.

What's wrong with that?
For one thing, you're ignoring people who might know a lot that would be useful in making the decision. You're accepting the idea that because you're in the CEO seat, you somehow know more or you're smarter than everyone else. But what

you're really doing is cutting yourself off from hearing options or ideas that might be better.

How do you create the kind of atmosphere where information flows freely?

You have to recognize that your position can be a hindrance to getting the best information. And so can your personality. My own greatest enemy is my personality—I can convince the people on my team of a point of view. I'm older than they are. I've done more research than they have. I know more than they do. I can influence them perhaps too much and therefore not get the best answers. So when we were doing the research for *Good to Great*, I built a culture that began with disagreements, that set people up to disagree with each other and disagree with me.

I tried to increase what I call my questions-to-statements ratio. I learned this from the *Good to Great* leaders we were studying. They were just marvelous at igniting dialogue and debate with Socratic questions. And I tried to make heroes out of those on my team who identified flaws in my thinking. At the next meeting I might say, "I really want to give Leigh or Brian or Stefanie credit. She really pushed my thinking, and I wasn't looking at this right."

I looked for people with a streak of irreverence and independent thought. One of my favorite researchers is a young man who went to Princeton, majored in medieval literature, and then joined the Marine Corps. Now, that's independent thinking. I wanted him on my team because he's not going to care what I think.

The really critical part came in designing the research so that for every piece of the puzzle—for every case, every analysis—someone on the team knows that piece as well as I do or better. This was a key mechanism to reduce the odds that my authority and strong personality would override the evidence.

Does having that kind of team make it harder to reach consensus?
I really want to underscore something. This is not about consensus.

You mean it depends on conflict?
That's the key. What we found in companies that make good decisions is the debate is real. When Colman Mockler at Gillette is trying to decide whether to go with cheaper, disposable plastic razors or more expensive ones, he asks marvelous questions. He's Socratic. He pushes people to defend their points of view. He lets the debate rage. And this is, by the way, not an isolated case. We found this process in all the companies we studied, when they made a leap to greatness. The debate is real. It is real, violent debate in search of understanding.

And then in the end, the leader makes the call?
Yes. It's conflict and debate leading to an executive decision. No major decision we've studied was ever taken at a point of unanimous agreement. There was always some disagreement in the air.

Doesn't that make it hard to carry out the decision?
Our research showed that before a major decision, you would see significant debate. But after the decision, people would unify behind that decision to make it successful. Again, and I can't stress this too much, it all begins with having the right people—those who can debate in search of the best answers but who can then set aside their disagreements and work together for the success of the enterprise.

"NO MAJOR DECISION THAT WE'VE
STUDIED WAS EVER TAKEN AT A POINT OF
UNANIMOUS AGREEMENT."

Okay, so creating a debate is crucial. What are some other ingredients of great decisions?

Most people start with the outside world and try to figure out, How do we adapt to it? Greatness doesn't happen that way. It starts with an internal drive. And there's a really key question with big decisions: What is the truth of this situation? There are three parts to this question. The first is internal: What are our real core values and our real aspirations? I mean, what do we really stand for? What do we really want to get done? What is internally driving us? I believe that it is the internal imprint that drives all the action. Everybody harps about "It's all about responding to the outside world." But the great companies are internally driven, externally aware.

"IT'S REALLY A STREAM OF DECISIONS OVER TIME, BRILLIANTLY EXECUTED, THAT ACCOUNTS FOR GREAT OUTCOMES."

—JIM COLLINS, *author of* Built to Last *and* Good to Great.

So the first question is, What is really driving us internally? The second question is, What is the truth about the outside world? And in particular, What is the truth about how it operates and how it is changing?

And the third question is, When you intersect our internal drive with external reality, what's the truth about what we can distinctively contribute potentially better than anyone else in the world?

Now, let's look at Boeing's decision to build the 707. What are the factors? First, you have the values of Boeing, which had to do with "We're adventurers, for goodness' sake. We like doing big, adventurous things. We'd rather not be in business than not do that." And second, the aspiration to make Boeing even greater than it was. Those are internal drives. They had nothing to do with adapting to the outside world.

But the second question—What was the truth about the outside world and how it was changing?—well, the war was over. There wasn't going to be as much demand for bombers. And there was a major change in technology, from propellers to jets. And the demand for military aircraft was going to decline relative to demand for commercial aircraft. So that's how the outside world was changing.

On to question No. 3: What could Boeing do better than anyone else in the world? Well, they had jet technology. They'd been building those big strato bombers, the B-47 and the B-52. They had experience, so they knew they could build a large-scale jet. Boeing confronted the truth, internal and external, and grasped that it could make a distinctive impact by bringing the world into the Jet Age—and that's when Bill Allen pulled the trigger on the 707.

We've been talking about big decisions, but there's a lot more to running a business than making one life-or-death decision, right?

No decision, no matter how big, is any more than a small fraction of the total outcome. Yes, some decisions are much bigger than others, and some are forks in the road. But as far as what determines outcomes, the big decisions are not like 60 of 100 points. They're more like six of 100 points. And there's a whole bunch of others that are like 0.6, or 0.006. They add up to a cumulative result. Business schools have regrettably taught us that it's all about the singular case decision. And when you and I write, we like the dramatic moment of decision.

Right. So-and-so leaned back in his chair, looked out the window, and said, "Should I do X or Y?"

But that's not the way life really happens. Yes, there are pivotal decisions, but it's really the stream of decisions over time, brilliantly executed, that accounts for great outcomes.

What elements of a leader's psychology, or the company's

psychology, affect decision-making?

One big factor is, Do you believe that your ultimate outcomes in life are externally determined—"I came from a certain family, I got the right job"? Or do you believe that how your life turns out is ultimately up to you, that despite all the things that happen, you are ultimately responsible for your outcomes?

Consider the airline industry, and think of all the events and factors outside managerial control that have hit it since 1972: fuel shocks, interest rate spikes, deregulation, wars, and 9/11. And yet the No. 1 performing company of all publicly traded companies in terms of return to investors for a 30-year period from 1972 to 2002 is an airline. According to *Money* magazine's retrospective look in 2002, Southwest Airlines beat Intel, Wal-Mart, GE—all of them! Now what would have happened if the folks at Southwest had said, "Hey, we can't do anything great because of our environment"? You could say, "Yeah, the airline industry is terrible. Everyone in it is statistically destined to lose money." But at Southwest they say, "We are responsible for our own outcomes."

Are you saying that you can control your own destiny with good decisions?

Not entirely. Luck is still a factor. But overall our research is showing that the primary factors reside more inside your control than outside. Yes, the world throws a lot at us, but the fundamental assumption needs to be like Southwest's—the ultimate responsibility for your destiny lies with you. The question is not what the world does to you but how you make an impact on the world. Decision-making is ultimately a creative act.

So it's hard to make good decisions if you don't really think they're going to make that much difference in the end. What else counts?

Our research shows one other variable to be vitally important for both the quality of decisions and their implementation. If you look at some of the great decisions in business history, the executives had the discipline to manage for the quarter-century, not the quarter. Look at Andy Grove deciding to abandon memory chips at Intel, Bill Allen and the Boeing 707, Reg Jones choosing Jack Welch to run GE, Darwin Smith selling the mills at Kimberly-Clark, Jim Burke standing firm in the Tylenol crisis, Tom Watson Jr. and the IBM 360. Those leaders were very clear that their ambition was for the long-term greatness of the company. And where decisions can go awry is when there's ambiguity or confusion about what you are really making decisions for—yourself or the company. Why should people throw their full creative energies into a decision that is ultimately about you?

Can you give us a preview of your current project?
My colleague Morten Hansen, formerly a professor at Harvard and now at Insead, and I conceived a simple question: Why do some prevail in brutally turbulent environments, while others do not? How do you retain control over your destiny when you are vulnerable to an environment that seeks to rip that control away from you or where you are statistically destined to fail? Think of it this way: If you wake up at Everest base camp and an unexpected storm hits, you'll probably be fine, but if you're high on the mountain when that storm hits, you just might die. Morten and I believe leaders increasingly feel they are high on the mountain, facing storms they never anticipated. We want to know, How do you build greatness anyway?

> "YOU CAN MAKE MISTAKES, EVEN SOME BIG MISTAKES, AND STILL PREVAIL. THAT'S A WONDERFUL THING TO KNOW."

And the answer is?
We're early in our research, and we don't yet know. But one thing we're learning is a great relief to me, because I'm so hard

on myself. You can make mistakes, even some big mistakes, and still prevail. That's a wonderful thing to know. You don't need a perfect hit rate. You might need to go four out of five on the really big ones, and there are some killer gotcha mistakes from which you can't recover, but you don't have to go five out of five. And I didn't know that before.

In the Heat of the Moment

by Michael Useem

The summer of '94 baked central Colorado in a heat rarely seen on the mountains; drought dried out the earth, leaving it gasping for moisture—and prone to ignition. On the morning of July 2, Storm King Mountain began to burn. By July 4 the resulting fire had spread to perhaps three acres, a relatively small and slow-moving blaze—and one, local officials decided, that could wait while they put out dozens of more serious ones.

It was not until the morning of July 5 that the first firefighters ventured up to contain it. Less than 36 hours later, 14 of them were dead. Elite members of a caste of itinerant warriors who battle in hardhats and chainsaws against one of humanity's oldest enemies, these ten men and four women were consumed by a wall of fire that moved almost 20 miles an hour.

The crisis on Storm King Mountain was not only a natural disaster, it was also the product of human actions. A firefighter named Don Mackey made several of the big decisions—some good, too many of them bad, at least one of them heroic. Mackey was a product—you might even say a victim—of a system that had failed to teach how to make good decisions. For years the agencies responsible for wild-land firefighting had focused on fire behavior rather than human behavior—akin to a business's concentrating on engineering rather than customers. Though earlier tragedies had often hinged on human error, the recommendations sent forth were usually technical. The result was that Mackey and others hit the mountain with state-of-the-art gear but scant training in how to make decisions under pressure.

As in most disasters, no single decision was responsible for the outcome on Storm King Mountain; instead, it was the result of a cascading series of smaller ones. One of the tragedies of Storm King is that the errors could have been avoided: Over-optimism. Untested assumptions. Unheeded warnings. Poor intelligence. Failure to clarify authority. The "collapse in decision-making" was "almost automatic," a U.S. Forest Service researcher argued afterward.

At NASA, it took a second space-shuttle explosion to convince the agency that its problems weren't just technical but also organizational. And it took Storm King Mountain to change the way forest fires are fought. Today wild-land firefighters are schooled extensively in how to make timely decisions under complex and stressful conditions. Trainees walk in the footsteps of Don Mackey. They pause at the spot where he yelled his final instruction. They sprint uphill while a stopwatch runs. They imagine what a wall of flame must look like when it's moving 20 miles an hour. And they often end up, panting, at a granite cross that marks the spot where Mackey fell—and near which his father camps every year to commemorate the anniversary of his son's death.

Normally, as a business-school professor, I do my research into leadership and management in more austere surroundings. But by examining nine key moments in the Storm King fire, I sought insight into what can inspire great decisions and poor ones. The decisions made by smokejumpers—parachuting firefighters—are unusually clear-cut and consequential. At root, however, they are not unlike decisions faced by managers. Faulty decisions helped bring down Enron and

WorldCom. Good decisions have driven the success of companies like eBay and Southwest.

With that in mind, and in the company of 17 wild-land firefighters, I walked the slopes of the 9,000-foot mountain, located 40 miles northwest of Aspen, to learn its lessons. More, I wanted to understand what conditions can help leaders make the right call, even under extreme circumstances. What follows is a reconstruction, drawn from interviews, research, and reports, of the events that led to one of the worst days in the history of wild-land firefighting.

As first light dawned on July 5, Butch Blanco, 50, a veteran firefighter with the U.S. Bureau of Land Management (BLM), hiked up Storm King Mountain to evaluate the situation. Just a few months before, Blanco had qualified as an incident commander, the person who takes charge of a fire. A former city firefighter, Blanco was known for giving a long leash to his crews when it came to getting the job done. (Blanco declined to speak with *Fortune*.)

Presently he and his team of seven began digging a line around the slow-moving fire. Using picks, shovels, and saws, they scraped the earth clean—one person rooting out the vegetation, another chucking it to the side. The idea was to create what is known as a fire line—a thin strip where the fire has nothing to feed on and thus cannot cross. But this blaze was more tenacious than Blanco expected, and at 8:19 a.m. he radioed for more help.

Since Blanco's fire was still not a priority—there were many bigger ones in the area—it was not until 5:20 p.m. that an eight-person crew of smokejumpers finally boarded a small plane. The jumper nearest the door was Don Mackey, 34. The father of two, Mackey had eight seasons of smokejumping under his belt and had also served as an instructor. Strong and well built, with the look of a mountain man, Mackey was regarded as a good smokejumper. Seated next to him was Sarah Doehring, a slightly built but tensile-strong woman from upstate New York whom Mackey had helped train. "He was easygoing, a likable guy, the kind of guy we enjoyed being around," she said of Mackey. And as a firefighter, "he was very competent." Doehring remembers thinking that it "could be difficult down there" but was reassured by her teammate's confident demeanor.

At 5:45 p.m. the smokejumpers left the plane. Because Mackey happened to be sitting in the seat nearest the door, he leaped and landed first. That made him, in accord with a protocol that interpreted "leadership" in the most literal sense, "jumper-in-charge." He would coordinate the landing and prepare the crew to go into fire combat; the fire itself was still Blanco's responsibility. Blanco and his crew, however, had trouble with their chainsaws and were unequipped for a night on the mountain. They descended to the town of Glenwood Springs for the evening.

The fire was not resting. The flames crossed the fire line Blanco's crew had cut, growing from 30 acres to 50. Mackey went into action against the blaze. "We all thought we were going to dig a line around it by midnight" to contain the fire, said Doehring. But it continued to spread, and Mackey realized he needed more firefighters. In Blanco's absence he took the initiative, radioing a request at 11:30 p.m. for two more crews.

The cold mountain ridge permitted only fitful rest. Wide awake at 2 a.m., Mackey worried that the fire was burning especially hot for that time of night. As dawn broke on July 6, he therefore asked for aerial surveillance (Decision 2), a fixed-wing aircraft that would serve as a full-time "eye in the sky." Officials informed Mackey that none was available; instead he got the services of a light helicopter that would have to do double duty ferrying gear as well as monitoring the fire. The effect was to leave him partially blind.

Early on the morning of July 6, Butch Blanco reappeared on the ridge with a crew of 11. In his absence, Mackey had made all the right moves: He'd tracked the fire vigilantly, secured more crew, and requested aerial intelligence. Now he and Blanco huddled. Deciding they needed better information before settling on a strategy, they boarded the helicopter at 9:30 a.m. to get a better sense of the fire. What they saw was worrisome. The blaze had expanded to 125 acres and was creeping down the west flank of the ridge. Mackey now proposed a bold plan. He wanted to cut a fire line very close to the flames—below them, since flames can climb a slope faster than a person can—on the west flank of the ridge. Before turning left and extending horizontally across the slope, the line would cut sharply down for its first 300 feet. The downward gradient reached 55 percent-a one-foot drop in elevation for every two feet forward—making for a tough return climb.

Blanco agreed with the strategy and Mackey prepared for action. In retrospect, this was a crucial moment in which two important things happened. First, Blanco effectively—though not officially—ceded some of his authority to Mackey, who became the point man on how to deal with the downhill fire line. And second, both men committed themselves to a strategy at odds with several established rules.

"Downhill-fire-line construction is hazardous in steep terrain, fast-burning fuels, or rapidly changing weather," warns the wild-land firefighters' manual. All three conditions prevailed in the canyon. The manual also cautions against relying on a steep uphill escape route. But since the crews were already on top of the ridge and could not readily redeploy to the bottom, cutting a downhill fire line seemed the pragmatic way to go.

Still, some of Mackey's team considered this a dangerous call. "You sure you want us to do that?" one radioed back. "Go down that side?" Mackey reaffirmed the decision, to be challenged again: "Are there any safe spots down there?" "It doesn't look too bad," Mackey responded. Again, his smoke-jumpers hesitated. "We're going to wait for you to come down here and explain some stuff to us," said one.

Face to face with his crew, Mackey noted that the vegetation became sparser down the hill. In any case, he argued, the fire would run back uphill—above the proposed fire line—in the unlikely event it surged out of control. "Let me have a big crew and we'll do this. We'll do fine," he said. Mackey's confidence got the crew moving. At 11:30 a.m., armed with saws, axes, and shovels, they began to cut and scrape a new fire line.

This moment of decision illustrates an important aspect of leadership dynamics. Seasoned urban firefighters, research shows, tend to break some firehouse rules between fires but go by the book during them. Beginners are more likely to stray. Don Mackey was serving as a de facto incident commander—something he had never done before. Butch Blanco was also new to command. In this regard they were both beginners, and as such they lacked the leadership experience that can build a robust sense that the worst can, in fact, happen. Standard operating procedures are intended to guard against just that, but there was no veteran in authority to insist on them.

An hour later eight more smokejumpers floated down onto the ridge. More than two dozen firefighters were now deployed on the ridge—Blanco's 11, Mackey's eight, and the eight newcomers. At 1 p.m. an elite team of "hotshots" from Oregon landed. With four different teams on the mountain, the question of who exactly was in charge was muddied. Mackey was now directly supervising 24 people, including the hotshots, over whom he had no authority, formal or otherwise. Was this his fire now, Mackey wondered? At 2 p.m. he asked fellow smokejumper Kevin Erickson whether he thought Butch Blanco was the incident commander or Mackey himself. "I don't know," Erickson responded. "Neither do I," said Mackey. But he took no steps to clarify the issue.

The lingering ambiguity may explain the reason no one posted a lookout. Under standard firefighting procedure, a crew leader must establish a lookout to ensure that no flames are burning below a fire line. Incident commanders are expected to be aware of the entire environment as it evolves. Acceptance of that responsibility here would have dictated the assignment of fire lookouts, radio contact with all parties, and checking out the situation personally. "Look up, down, and around" exhorts the fire manual.

When authority becomes diffused or confused, the chances of a crucial matterbeing overlooked rise sharply. In the event, Mackey's view of the fire line was blocked by a vertical cleavage known as Lunchspot Ridge. Concealed beyond that ridge, the fire had already burned down below the level of the fire line. Had there been a well-posted lookout-or the surveillance plane Mackey never got—the radios would have been crackling with warnings.

Because Blanco concentrated on controlling the fire at the top of the ridge and Mackey on completing the fire line lower down, neither had an overall view of the developing situation. Thus neither sensed that the canyon could be on the cusp of a blowup—a rare phenomenon when a fire suddenly bursts across the landscape. Exploding in seconds, the blowup "is one of nature's most powerful forces, equivalent to a mighty storm, avalanche, or volcanic eruption," writes John Maclean in *Fire on the Mountain*, a book on the Storm King disaster. "It can sweep away in moments everything before it, the works of nature and of humankind, and sometimes humankind itself."

Unbeknownst to the crews, nature was brewing one more dangerous element. The local meteorologist predicted that a cold front would surge through around 3 p.m., generating no rain but plenty of wind. Due to bureaucratic bungling, the message never arrived—and Mackey did not ask for it. No warning light flashed in the back of his mind from prior experience or training to alert him to the risk of a missing weather forecast. These two decisions—not to clarify his leadership responsibilities and not to ask for weather updates—were closely connected. If Mackey had felt certain that he was in charge, he might have felt compelled to seek the data—and then he would have known to protect those on the fire line from the anticipated currents.

At 3:30 p.m., Mackey took note of the rising winds, and he

assigned Sarah Doehring to patrol the west flank fire line for burning debris and hot spots. He also sat a few minutes with her for a bite to eat. Though outwardly relaxed, he had much on his mind. "What should I do if the wind comes up?" asked Doehring. "Go down," he instructed. As they stood up, Doehring began to resume her patrol toward the far end of the fire line, when Mackey changed his mind and ordered her back to the top of the ridge. Feeling tense about the worsening conditions, Doehring was relieved to turn around—an act that saved her life. Most of the other firefighters on the fire line remained working between 1,450 to 1,880 feet from the ridge top.

By 4 p.m., smoke swirled, flames churned, air thundered—all the classic signs of a blowup. A 1998 Forest Service analysis said, "The fire began burning through the live fuel canopy as a continuous flaming front." The front came surging from both below and the far end of the fire line. In an instant Mackey stopped fighting the fire and raced to survive it. Grasping the acute danger, he instructed eight nearby firefighters to run directly up Lunchspot Ridge to an area where he knew there was sufficient ground cover to serve as a safe zone. "Go up!" he shouted. "There's good black farther up." They would find the "good black" and survive by huddling inside their portable fire shelters.

Mackey himself did not run up to safety. Instead he dashed back along the fire line to rush the firefighters still there across the line toward safety. He radioed ahead: "Okay, everybody out of the canyon!" In running back across the fire line-rather than directly up Lunchspot Ridge—Mackey had taken the leader's ultimate decision. At a moment when his self-preservation must have screamed, "Run up!" he instead returned to assist those most in peril.

At Mackey's urging, six firefighters crested the ridge top with seconds to spare. One of them, author Sebastian Junger recounts in *Fire*, was Brad Haugh. "The fire blew up behind a little ridge below me," Haugh reported. "People were yelling into their radios, 'Run! Run! Run!' I was roughly 150 feet from the top of the hill, and the fire got there in ten or 12 seconds. I made it over the top and just tumbled and rolled down the other side, and when I turned around, there was just this incredible wall of flame."

Mackey and the rest were not far behind, but the steepness of the hill meant that they were not moving fast—perhaps one to three feet per second. The fire, meanwhile, was coming at nine feet per second. At 4:16 it caught up with them. A surging 300-foot wall of flame overtook nine of the Oregon hotshots and three smokejumpers, including Mackey. They were less than 100 yards short of safety.

It took five more days to bring the fire under control. The final death toll was 14 (two died elsewhere on the mountain), making it one of the deadliest forest fires in U.S. history.

Six months later, Ted Putnam, a researcher with the U.S. Forest Service, wrote a paper on the tragedy. Putnam did not hesitate to affix blame-but none of it was directed at the fire-fighters themselves. It was directed at the committee that had released the official report. Their recommendations had focused on the technical aspects of fighting a fire, such as developing better fuel inventories, improved weather forecasting, and more accurate fire prediction. "These tried-and-true solutions," Putnam wrote, "simply fail to deal with a major cause of the fatalities. We lost firefighters on Storm King Mountain because decision processes naturally degraded. At this time we do not have training courses that give firefighters the knowledge to counter these processes."

Today that is no longer true. There is a weeklong course, Incident Leadership, designed for veteran wild-land firefighters. Emergencies are simulated, roles assigned, and performance evaluated, sometimes harshly, by peers and experts. Would-be incident commanders are taught how to construct a safe fire line, detect decision errors, and cope with ambiguous authority. It is the course Don Mackey should have taken-but it did not then exist.

ANATOMY OF A TRAGEDY

It started as a routine forest fire; there were dozens of more serious blazes in Colorado in the drought-ridden summer of '94. But Storm King ended up as the deadliest. Smokejumper Don Mackey made nine key decisions on that terrible day.

16.5 HOURS
Decision #1 - *At 11:30 p.m. on July 5, with the fire intensifying, Don Mackey radios a request for two more firefighting crews.*

10.5 HOURS
#2 - *Around dawn on July 6, Mackey asks for continuous aerial surveillance of the fire. The request is denied.*

6.5 HOURS
#3 - *At 9:30 a.m., Mackey and Butch Blanco, leader of another crew, conduct their own reconnaissance in a helicopter assigned to the fire.*

6 HOURS
#4 - *Mackey proposes to cut a fire line below the flames on the west flank of the ridge —a risky strategy to which Blanco agrees.*

2 HOURS
#5 - *Mackey wonders who is in command but does not clarify the situation. One possible result: No lookout is posted.*

1.5 HOURS
#6 - *A local weather forecast predicts strong winds but no rain; Mackey does not receive or ask for the forecast.*

30 MIN.
#7 - *Mackey orders Sarah Doehring to the top of the main ridge. Thanks to this order, she survives.*

16 MIN.
#8 - *Sensing an imminent blowup, Mackey directs eight firefighters to Lunchspot Ridge. They all survive.*

0 MIN.
#9 - *The fire blows up and Mackey, only 100 feet from the Lunchspot, decides to risk his own life to hurry the 18-member crew working along the west flank fire line to safety on the main ridge.*

The rules are different too. No longer is the first smoke-jumper on the ground automatically in charge; now it is the most experienced person. And firefighters are trained to refuse excessive risk. The lesson that the fire services took away-and from which others can learn-is that how decisions are made affects the quality of the decisions. Don Mackey had only ambiguous authority and little training. Still, he took charge and made in his final moments swift decisions that saved lives. His sacrifice is now instructing a new generation of fire leaders on how to make the right decisions when lives depend on them.

Great
ROLE MODELS

*Let Leaders Who Break the
Mold Be Your Inspiration*

GREAT ROLE MODELS

Let Leaders Who Break the Mold Be Your Inspiration

The most valued traits in managers, especially if they're approaching the highest levels, are not entirely what they were five or ten years ago. Obviously they still have to deliver knockout results. It's how they do it that's changing. Tom Neff, the SpencerStuart headhunter who is one of the world's top CEO recruiters, says, "The style for running a company is different from what it used to be. Companies don't want dictators, kings, or emperors." Instead of someone who gives orders, they want someone who asks probing questions that force the team to think and find the right answers—"a subtle technique," Neff says. Reinforcing that view is a new survey from Right Management Consultants, a major outplacement firm. It finds that the No. 1 skill companies seek in managers is "ability to motivate and engage others." Ranking a close second is ability to communicate, a trait Neff's clients also increasingly want. Standout leaders should additionally have on-the-ground operating experience outside the U.S. and they'll need megawatts of energy to meet the demands of global travel and a 24/7 world. —BY GEOFFREY COLVIN

MASTERING
THE ART OF DISRUPTION

By Fred Vogelstein

The Master of Disruption is at it again. With his two remarkable companies—Apple Computer and animated movie house Pixar—dominating the headlines, Steve Jobs finds himself in the kind of position that most mad-genius tech wunderkinds can only fantasize about: thrilling consumers while wreaking havoc in multiple industries. Apple sold 100 iPods a minute in the fourth quarter of 2005, and its iTunes Music Store could account for 10 percent of all music sales in the U.S. in 2006. It's only fitting that the release in mid-January 2006 of a new line of superfast Mac computers featuring Intel chips came just as Apple's market cap briefly passed that of rival Dell. The company turned 30 on April 1, 2006. Happy birthday, Apple.

The news about Pixar is, if anything, more dramatic. When word broke that the movie house might link up with Disney—and that Jobs himself might join the media behemoth's leadership team—jaws dropped from Wall Street to Hollywood to Silicon Valley. When the deal closed and Jobs sold Pixar to Disney, he arguably became the most powerful investor in entertainment. His head start on digital animation combined with his burgeoning iEmpire places him squarely in the intersection of Hollywood and high tech—the one figure in position to control the fast-moving evolution of media consumption.

How he got here may be boiled down to one simple reality: Jobs has proven himself unrivaled in the art of managing disruption. Many entrepreneurs talk about turning ideas into products that change the world. Yet the landscape is littered with first movers who ended up finishing last. In so many cases, being out in front just makes you a target for deep-pocketed rivals. Think back to the early PC manufacturers or the spreadsheet- and word-processing-software makers. Can you recall any of them? Does VisiCalc ring a bell? XyWrite? Probably not. But Microsoft's Excel and Word are still with us. What about portals and search engines? Pioneers like Alta Vista, Lycos, and Excite got steamrollered by Google. More recently NetFlix and TiVo have created hugely popular new businesses in the realm of movies and television, but they are in peril of being usurped by cheaper digital video recorders from cable operators and video-on-demand. Research in Motion's BlackBerry brand has become the Kleenex for remote e-mail, yet the company must shudder at the introduction of each new multifunction cellphone.

At both Apple and Pixar, Jobs has been able to simultaneously harness technology in a way that throws the status quo into disorder and ride that chaos to the front of the pack. What's more, he's established two different models for how to do it. Apple's trick has been not just its game-changing tech breakthroughs (music and computers made easy) but its relentless push to disrupt itself before others have a chance to do so. "The thing that most people don't realize about Steve is that he is not only really good at taking technology and turning it into good-looking, easy-to-use products, he's really good at doing it faster than anyone else," says Paul Saffo of the Institute of the Future in Palo Alto. Think about the iPod here: The first one released four years ago had a monochrome screen and a five-gigabyte hard drive. Now it has a color screen and a 60-gigabyte hard drive at roughly the same price. What other business would obsolete a successful product like the iPod mini after only 18 months to introduce the nano?

With Pixar, Jobs has taken a different tack: co-opting the competition. For many disruptors, it works the other way around: The established players eventually crank themselves up, throw big dollars at a new area, and swamp an upstart. Instead Pixar exploited a moment of maximum leverage—when Disney's animation business was lackluster and its lucrative distribution deal with Pixar was up for renegotiation—to step inside a potentially big competitor. In the process, Jobs got an even bigger landscape to gallop across—and a much bigger horse. Imagine the possibilities for disruption with the resources of both Apple and Disney at his disposal. Overnight the iPod has gotten deeper access to ESPN as well as the entire library of Disney films and ABC television shows. Can you feel the tremors?

WHAT MAKES GE GREAT?

By Geoffrey Colvin

On paper, the most admired company in America—and the world—may not look all that distinguished. It isn't the biggest or the most profitable; it's not the fastest growing or the most valuable. Its stock has been practically inert for years. Allegations of managed quarterly earnings keep showing up in the press. What's to admire?

Yet this company, General Electric, is No. 1 on our list once again in 2006, the most admired company for the sixth time in the past decade. (It last reached the top slot in 2002.) And if you're wondering whether we've got some pro-GE bias in our survey—nope. GE has also ranked No. 1 in the *Financial Times'* "most respected" survey for seven of the past eight years, and it topped a recent Barron's ranking of most admired companies. The results speak for themselves. But why does the world love this company so much?

The answer lies in the fact that our survey (like the others) is a poll not of consumers but of businesspeople working in the same hard world as GE. They admire GE the way golf pros voted Tiger Woods Player of the Year in 2003, when he didn't win a major championship or top the money list: Through good years and bad, GE consistently does things the rest only wish they could.

For the past century or so, for example, GE has continually set the agenda of management ideas and practices that other companies will follow. Practically everyone in business realizes this. GE's record of being ahead of the game is remarkable. Under Charles Coffin, who led the firm from 1892 to 1912, GE set principles of organizational design that would guide large companies—above all, the idea that the company's most important product was not light bulbs or transformers but managerial talent. In 1900 the company started the first corporate R&D lab, and in the 1930s it focused on cooperative labor relations, adopting pension plans and profit-based bonuses to keep employees away from unions. In the 1950s it produced the famous "blue books"—five volumes of ultra-detailed guidance for GE managers—that shaped management everywhere. In the 1960s it led the move to strategic planning. In the 1980s and 1990s, it took concepts like leadership development, Work Out, and Six Sigma and made them the stuff of the global management culture. Most organizations will never establish any kind of intellectual leadership. Maintaining it for 100 years is a unique achievement.

But wait a minute. A lot of those ideas are dead. Isn't strategic planning now generally scorned, for example? Aren't the blue books and the whole centralizing ethos behind them long since abandoned? Yes—and GE led the scorning and abandoning. Here is another GE trait that businesspeople especially admire: an ability to change direction unabashedly. "Most people inside GE learn from the past but have a healthy disrespect for history," says CEO Jeff Immelt. "They have an ability to live in the moment and not be burdened by the past, which is extremely important."

It's hard to find any other organization that so enthusiastically destroys its own creations. Coffin created an organizational structure based on functions; Ralph Cordiner (CEO, 1950-63), broke it to pieces. He got GE into computers, and then Fred Borch (CEO, 1963-72) bailed out. Reg Jones (CEO, 1972-81) established a layer of sector executives and bought a coal-mining company; Jack Welch (1981-2001) abolished the layer and sold the mines. Welch built up the insurance business; Immelt offloaded it. Immelt is putting his own stamp on the company by reemphasizing its scientific research labs and a long-dormant marketing function.

The result of GE's seamless, constant reinvention of itself is that while companies are constantly emulating GE, they're frequently a step or more behind, and they know it. That's another reason they consistently admire the company.

GE does one more big thing: develop people, evaluate them, and act on the results. The company takes a lot of heat for getting rid of the bottom 10 percent of its employees every year, but that's only the end point of a process of constant appraisal. The fired ones are not surprised when the ax comes down. And the result is an extraordinarily high-performing organization. "The ability to demand high performance without being heartless," says Immelt, "has been a part of GE for a long time."

Dan Mudd is the president and CEO of Fannie Mae; as president and CEO of GE Capital Japan from 1999 to mid-2005, he saw this dynamic from the inside. "GE, like anywhere else, has a little bit of politics, a little bit of personal stuff, and all that," he says, "but compared with all the other organizations I know, it's minimized. It's upfront. You know what you have to do to succeed." Most companies, frankly, don't have the stomach to give frequent, rigorous evaluations —and to fire those who need to be fired. They admire a company that does.

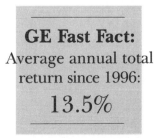

GE Fast Fact:
Average annual total return since 1996:
13.5%

But then there's the matter of

the stock price, down about 18 percent since Immelt took over in September 2001. In the view of one fan who knows a bit about the market, GE's recent lassitude in that regard isn't so important. Warren Buffett says, "I think the people who respond to *Fortune's* survey are looking beyond the recent action of the stock—looking at the challenges Jeff has faced and how well he is handling them." Of course, a flailing stock is nothing to admire. The fact that GE's reputation has stayed so solid despite the stock's woes probably reflects a belief among those surveyed that GE will rise again.

It's all about the long term. No other U.S. company has been as dominant for as long as GE. Of the 12 firms that Charles Dow put into his original Dow Jones industrial average in 1896, GE is the only one still in the index, and most of the others are dead. Survival is another achievement to admire.

Could GE blow it? Sure. All it would take is a slight slackening of rigor, a tiny easing of standards, a growing taste for self-congratulation, and GE could go the way of Woolworth, Studebaker, and Bethlehem Steel.

Immelt quite properly says, "I would never run the company to be the most admired." But because GE's stature is based on so much more than just a good year or two, alarm bells should go off in Fairfield, Conn., if it isn't at least in contention.

GENENTECH:
THE BEST PLACE TO WORK NOW

By Betsy Morris

D omagoj Vucic didn't come to Genentech for the rich stock
options or the free cappuccino or the made-to-order sushi
or the parties every Friday night. He came from the University
of Georgia seven years ago because he believed Genentech could
help him answer a burning question: What is it that keeps caterpillars infected with baculovirus alive for an entire seven days
before they explode into a gooey puddle? Figuring that one
out could, believe it or not, be a big step toward curing cancer.

Doctor-scientist Napoleone Ferrara didn't come for the
perks either. He joined Genentech in 1988 because the company would allow him to pursue an obsession: the study of the
formation of blood vessels that feed, say, a tumor, and the
search for an antibody to disrupt the process.

It's not just the bioscientists. Ask Cynthia Wong, a mother
of two, why she chose to settle at Genentech after working at
Citibank and Towers Perrin, and she doesn't even mention the
onsite day care or the concierge service that can pull off a
birthday party on a moment's notice. Instead the senior manager quotes a breast-cancer patient who had visited her sales
department a day earlier. "She has two little girls," Wong says,
getting tears in her eyes all over again. "She wants to see them
in braces. She wants to be there when they pick out their prom
dresses." With the help of a Genentech drug called Herceptin,
she probably will.

Work that really matters—it's what makes Genentech the
Best Company to Work For in 2006. But there's plenty else to

like about this low-key, high-tech biotech located just north of San Francisco International Airport. For starters, 29-year-old Genentech is not just the very first biotech; it's the brightest star in a promising industry that has chronically under-delivered. The company's 2005 revenues should come to $6.6 billion, according to Wall Street estimates, triple what Genentech pulled in four years ago. Its stock price has doubled in 2005, to $95 a share. At one point in December 2005 it had a market cap of $102 billion, making it the 20th-most-valuable company in the U.S., ahead of Merck, Lilly, and every other pharmaceutical company except Johnson & Johnson and Pfizer. "There is only one drug company that has really come from nowhere to be a major force in this industry, and that is Genentech," says Peter Tollman, a senior vice president and biopharmaceutical expert at Boston Consulting Group. "It is the only drug company in the world that has created that much value without a merger."

> GENENTECH HAS A LOT IN COMMON WITH TWO OTHER BAY AREA SUPERSTARS: GOOGLE AND APPLE.

Genentech's secret, anybody here will tell you, is its culture. And that is what has propelled the company to the top of this year's list. With its storybook view of San Francisco Bay, the place feels more like a college campus than a pillar of the Fortune 500. Signs point to the North Campus, down by the water, and the South Campus, up on the hill. Employees don't get assignments, they get "appointments." They traverse the grounds by shuttle bus and bicycles provided by the company. Every Friday night there's at least one "ho-ho"—Genentechese for kegger—a tradition that began in the '70s when the workforce was mostly a handful of rowdy postdocs barely out of grad school. At Genentech, every milestone calls for a party and a commemorative T-shirt—and on very big occasions, very big celebrity bands. In 2004, after an unusual run of FDA approvals, the parking lot in front of Building 9 became the site of a rock concert featuring Elton John, Mary J. Blige, and Matchbox 20.

All this would be way too dot com to make business sense if it weren't for another performer who took the stage that day—and who got about as much applause as the bands. That would be Art Levinson, Genentech's impish, brilliant scientist CEO, dressed for the occasion in tennis shoes and a black CLONE OR DIE T-shirt. The 55-year-old Levinson, who once bet his colleagues that five of them could fit inside an ice machine (they did), has made mostly right bets for the company ever since he took the helm in 1995—championing its science, creating a stream of new drugs, and winning over employees by making clear to all that there would be no butt-covering culture at Genentech.

In fact, Genentech's culture has a whole lot in common with those of two other Bay Area superstars, Google and Apple. All three imbue employees with idealism. Apple keeps a laserlike focus on the customer. Google's motto is DO NO EVIL. Genentech's: IN BUSINESS FOR LIFE. All three companies flout conventional wisdom and take a damn-the-torpedoes approach to naysayers. All three know one another well. Levinson is on the boards of Google and Apple; he and Steve Jobs are often seen hanging out at Genentech, deep in discussion. (Google hasn't been around long enough to qualify as a 100 Best Companies to Work for candidate; Apple declined to participate in the survey.) And all three put huge emphasis on attracting the best and the brightest. Genentech awards sabbaticals to stave off burnout. To keep creativity alive, both it and Google encourage their scientists and engineers to spend fully 20 percent of each workweek pursuing pet projects. Many corporations think it's terribly cutting-edge to maintain an arm's-length relationship with employees. These guys want you to move in.

Of course, it's easy to be a generous, enlightened employer when profits are flowing and your stock seems to have nowhere to go but up. IBM was that way for decades, once. But the awful mathematical truth—you don't need a Ph.D. to figure it out—is that high growth at this rate can't last forever.

Says David Botstein, former head of Genentech research and now a professor of genomics at Princeton: "At some point, someone, maybe Art, maybe his successor, is going to have to figure out how to transition Genentech into a steady-state company." Levinson says he won't worry about growth slowing until sometime after 2010. Right now, with the company averaging 151 new employees a month, he says, "The thing I worry about most is managing our growth." And protecting Genentech's mission, focus, and culture. "It's much easier to get alignment when you have fewer people."

Since the day the company was founded in 1976, Genentech's culture has been its competitive advantage. Founders Bob Swanson, a 29-year-old venture capitalist who studied the power of teams at MIT, and Herb Boyer, a pioneer gene splicer from the University of California at San Francisco, knew the success of their venture depended on luring and keeping big-brain bioscience talent. Within two years Genentech had concocted human insulin, which in 1982 became the first biotech drug to go to market. The company turned its first profit in 1979, the year before it went public, and has remained profitable ever since—despite a close call in the late 1980s, when it lost focus and stopped introducing new drugs, and the stock price flagged badly enough to make the company a takeover target. (Swiss drug giant Roche took a majority stake in 1990 and has let Genentech run independently ever since.) When Levinson was tapped to become CEO in 1995, Wall Street was skeptical but insiders cheered. Levinson was head of research, a top scientist, and astute at making calls on people and R&D.

During his first two years as CEO, Levinson persuaded the board to plow 50 percent of revenues back into research. (You read that number right. It's why, he believes, four of the company's 13 drugs are less than three years old, 30 more drugs are in the pipeline, and all eight of its clinical trials last year were successful.) He also decided to focus the company's science on "significant unmet needs" in the fields of oncology, immunology, and tissue growth and repair. He got rid of projects (and people) that didn't fit the program and forced fiefdoms like product development and basic research to work closely together. To head drug development, he tapped Susan Desmond-Hellmann, who had begun her career as an oncologist and has never forgotten what it's like to tell a young mother with breast cancer that she has run out of options. (Desmond-Hellmann is now president.)

Genentech pours tremendous energy into hiring people with that kind of passion. In fact, it can take five or six visits and 20 interviews to snag a job. The process is meant partly to screen out the free agents—people preoccupied with salary, title, and personal advancement. If candidates ask too many such questions, "Boom, wrong profile," says Levinson. The gantlet is also designed to let job candidates know exactly what they're getting themselves into. "We're extremely nonhierarchical," Levinson says. "We're not wearing ties. People don't call us doctor. We don't have special dining rooms." (They aren't even assigned parking spaces, and it's hell in the morning to find a spot.) Executive job seekers from Big Pharma, especially, find that a jolt, he says. "A lot of them say, 'But I like being different! I like being special!' Well, you're not going to be special here. If that's important to you, that's fine. But you won't be happy here."

Genentech looks for people who are wired like Ellen Filvaroff, a senior scientist in molecular oncology. Her walls are decorated with pictures of her patents and her toddler—side by side. The perks she likes most are little things—like being able to buy birthday cards and stamps and to mail packages from the company store. But the biggest kick by far, she says, is having colleagues who can help you crack the science more quickly. Collaboration is easy and encouraged. Once, when Filvaroff wasn't sure how to set up an experiment, she caught Napoleone Ferrara in the walkway between buildings 10 and 11. By the time they reached the doorway Filvaroff had refined her thinking enough to conduct the experiment, which turned into a published paper. Encounters like that, she says, "just bootstrap my science." As a mother of a young child, she's the least likely person to attend ho-hos. But the interplay of bioscience and brewski makes for unusually rewarding keggers, so she goes when she can.

Here status is conveyed not by snagging the fanciest title or the biggest office (CEO Levinson's measures about 9 feet by 12 feet and is done up with low-end metal office furniture). It's defined by matching wits and taking chances. Or seeing who can take the dare. At Genentech nobody dresses up, except on Halloween. On Halloween in 2005, Desmond-Hellmann spent the day as Snow White, and Levinson and the rest of the management team dressed as the Six Dwarfs (minus Dopey). They were en route to hand out candy at another office across town when their SUV convoy drove by archrival Amgen. Levinson hailed the driver to stop and told the group he wanted to have their picture taken on the Amgen front lawn, posed around the Amgen sign. They did, but Levinson was not entirely satisfied. What he really wanted, he told them, was a picture of Snow White and the Dwarfs inside the Amgen lobby. Some of the Dwarfs chickened out, and Snow White was about to—until Levinson goaded her. "Oh come on, Sue, don't be a weenie." They entered through the revolving doors and got a shot before security guards began to arrive and they had to abort and flee. "We know the names of our patients, and a lot of them die, and I think that's part of our loopiness," explains Walter Moore, VP of government affairs.

Like Apple and Google, Genentech, despite the fun and games, is anything but relaxed. Once or twice a year, staff scientists and researchers must defend their work before the Research Review Committee, the group of 13 Ph.D.s that decides how to allot the research budget. Some find the experience nerve-wracking, and that's okay, says Levinson. "I don't want people terrified, but it should not be a cakewalk either." The rigor is designed to vet the science, uncover the flaws, avoid the dead ends, and sift out politics and favoritism, so that in the end Levinson and Desmond-Hellmann have enough information to place the right bets on the research that will most likely lead to an actual drug. Sometimes scientists fail, or the work isn't deemed sufficiently high priority, and the RRC puts an end to a project. In those cases, not only are the researchers not fired; they usually have a say in their next assignment.

True innovation takes guts. Industrywide, new drugs on average cost about $800 million and take up to 12 years to develop. More than 90 percent of the drugs in clinical development never reach the market, including half of those that make it to late-stage clinical trials. That's why so many big drug companies are running out of new drugs. For a long time it was easier and lucrative enough to pursue what Vishva Dixit, vice president of research, calls the "detergent" strategy—creating me-too drugs in big established markets as if they were laundry soap, and then spending big bucks on marketing to steal share from rival pharmas.

At Genentech, using market data or return-on-investment analysis to drive the science is strictly taboo. "At the end of the day, we want to make drugs that really matter," says Levinson. "That's the transcendent issue." Not that this company considers itself a philanthropy. By decade's end, it aims to be the leading U.S. oncology company in terms of sales and a leader in both immunology and tissue-growth disorders, setting ambitious new product goals in each of those categories. It has a sales force of fewer than 1,000 and licenses with Roche and others to sell its products overseas.

Levinson really believes that if the company does the right thing, sales will follow. The strategy: Fund enough basic research in targeted areas of interest, and the results will yield multiple drugs—or drugs that can be used in multiple ways. That makes Genentech an especially rewarding place to work for a scientist like Ferrara, whose 17-year obsession—launched with a breakthrough made on discretionary time—led him to discover VEGF, a key to blood-vessel formation, which in turn enabled Genentech to develop an antibody that can choke off the blood supply to certain tumors. Those discoveries laid the groundwork for two of Genentech's newest drugs, Avastin, approved to treat colorectal cancer, and Lucentis, which is awaiting FDA approval for treatment of age-related blindness. Avastin might have died a premature death when it failed clinical trials three years ago, causing the company's share price to plunge nearly 10 percent overnight (to a split-adjusted $14.45 a share). But because Levinson and his lieutenants were so deep into the science, they knew better than to give up. Avastin, approved in February 2004, had sales of $774 million in the first nine months of 2005.

HIS ABHORRENCE OF CORPORATE-SPEAK HELPS
EXPLAIN WHY CEO LEVINSON LOATHES
CONSULTANTS. "THEY SUCK YOU DRY," HE SAYS.

Ferrara is studying VEGF alternatives for regulating blood supply that could lead to still more new drugs. And Domagoj Vucic's work that began with caterpillars has opened an area of anticancer research so promising that an executive calls it the company's "search for the Holy Grail." It involves an effort to regulate apoptosis, the natural ability of cells to self-destruct when they've lived out their lives or are stricken with disease. For Vucic the quest is personal: His friend and mentor at the University of Georgia, who helped launch the research, died of melanoma not long after Vucic left there. It is the kind of long-term, high-risk research that makes Genentech employees proud—and glad, they say, that they aren't at Big Pharma.

Scoffing at Big Pharma may be both great sport and an effective rallying cry, but everybody here is painfully aware that Genentech also runs the risk of getting too large. By the end of 2006, 40 percent of the workforce will have spent less than three years at Genentech; another 40 percent of its managers will be new to their positions. So the company is working furiously to acculturate the rookies. New-hire orientation includes patient lectures, history lessons by Boyer and other old-timers, in-depth sessions on the company's goals, its science—and the fact that the place works "because of all the thousands of little decisions that are made every day," says HR vice president Denise Smith-Hams. The company polls its workers weekly to ferret out complaints and monitor whether all the new parties are aligned with Genentech's goals.

When Levinson sees signs of culture atrophy, he pounces, as he did in an e-mail to senior managers in December of 2005 about "the spread of unintelligible, gibberish-laden PowerPoint presentations.... I have recently sat through several presentations that were simply incomprehensible—mind-numbing, bloated discourses that were full of buzzwords and otherwise devoid of meaningful content. This is a serious problem, and the worst part is that it's spreading like the disease it is." (His abhorrence of corporate-speak helps explain why Levinson loathes consultants. "They suck you dry," he says.)

In case the memo alone doesn't do the trick, Levinson invented a game called gBuzz Bingo. Here's how to play: From the company intranet, download a bingo card featuring terms like "actionable," "traction," "value-added," and "win-win." Take the card to any meeting where you expect the worst. Check off boxes as the words are uttered. First to complete a line wins, which of course requires that you shout out: "gBuzz!" The winner receives the smug satisfaction of silencing the b.s. And DNA by the Bay, as Genentechers call their company, keeps its magic—for one more meeting, at least.

THE EDUCATION OF ANDY GROVE

By Richard S. Tedlow

In 1991, an instructor at Stanford's Graduate School of Business presented his class with a case study. It went like this: A CEO was scheduled to address a major industry gathering, and he could give one of three speeches. The first would publicly commit his company to incorporating a sexy, sophisticated new technology in its products. The second speech would reaffirm the company's commitment to developing its existing technology. The third speech would do neither, leaving the decision to "the market." The stakes were enormous: A wrong decision could well ruin the business. What should the CEO do? The question was more than academic, because the CEO described in the case was also the man at the front of the classroom. Dr. Andrew S. Grove, like professor Indiana Jones, was better known for his exploits as "Andy," the famous leader of Intel Corp. But unlike Indy, Grove wasn't simply biding time here between adventures. His question was meant not just to challenge students' thinking but to advance his own. That big speech was three weeks away, and Grove had yet to make up his mind. He didn't know the answer.

It's not common for any CEO to stand before an audience and say, "I don't know what to do. What do you think?" It's even less common for that CEO to listen to the responses and take them seriously. But Grove, 69, has never lost track of the truth: that Intel has always been one wrong answer away from disaster—and that a closed mind is a trap door to the abyss.

Grove and Intel are now embedded so deeply inside our minds, our computers, and our culture—the man has been on 77 magazine covers, by one count—that with hindsight, their success seems foreordained. But the opposite is the case: By all odds, Intel should have failed. It should have been destroyed by the same brutal international competition that has killed apparel companies, tire companies, and television companies, or fallen into obscurity like Zilog and other successful chipmakers. Intel, too, should have stumbled on the terrifying treadmill of Moore's Law, which requires betting billions upon billions of dollars on ever more costly factories to make chips you're still developing for customers who've yet to demand them. It should have been eclipsed by an upstart competitor with a better mousetrap. Intel's success should never have happened—it was an anomaly, an outlier, a freak.

That's why Grove had chosen himself as the day's case study in the class he was teaching with Professor Robert Burgelman, his longtime collaborator and the author of *Strategy Is Destiny*. In business you often don't see the cliff until you've already walked over it. Visibility on the ground is bad, and the roadmap—well, that can't be trusted either. To spot the next cliff, Andy Grove was willing to let go of his instincts—since they could be wrong—and view himself as a student might: from outside, peering down with the wide-angle, disinterested perspective of the observer. Did the man below seem aware of his surroundings? Was he choosing the correct path? Was there a 1,000-foot drop ahead?

Normally, our society observes a division of labor. Musicians don't critique, and critics don't compose. Quarterbacks decide on Sunday, and fans deride on Monday. It is the singular ability to inhabit both roles at once—subject and object, actor and audience, master and student—that sets Grove apart. And it's why, for everything that has been written by and about him, we have yet to appreciate his biggest legacy. Andy Grove is America's greatest student and teacher of business.

By analyzing the decisions he made on the road to becoming a great leader, you can learn to hone your own leadership skills. Because there's no gain in being able to recruit great employees, handle a board, dazzle Wall Street, or rally your cavalry for a glorious charge at dawn's early light if you haven't figured out which way to point the horses.

Grove's output as a teacher of management has been prodigious. He has taught from the lectern, in the op-ed pages, in his famous (sometimes feared) one-on-one sessions, and with his books, including 1983's *High Output Management* and 1996's *Only the Paranoid Survive*, whose title entered the lexicon along with its phrase "strategic inflection point," which Grove defines as "a time in the life of a business when its fundamentals are about to change." His teaching would have been an impressive career in itself. Yet it is one thing to search for truth in the ivory tower and quite another to take those lessons, however wrenching, and apply them to a living, breathing business like Intel. Grove's most powerful lessons have been in the doing.

What can others learn from Grove's odyssey? As we face a future where change is not only constant but accelerating, reality will transform itself more swiftly than most humans—or most companies—are hard-wired to handle. Even startups that overturn one reality are easily overturned by the next big change. Grove has escaped natural selection by doing the evolving himself. Forcibly adapting himself to a succession of new realities, he has left a trail of discarded assumptions in his wake. When reality has changed, he has found the will to let go and embrace the new.

It's a performance as remarkable as his life story. There will not be another CEO who survived both the Nazis and the communists before becoming a naturalized capitalist. And yet Grove is the best model we've got for doing business in the 21st century. If you hope to thrive in an environment of rapid change, it is this outlier—his strengths forged in a distant and vanished world—that you should follow. Begin your lesson in leadership the same way Andy Grove attacks a problem: by setting aside everything you know.

As a historian whose subjects have been, until now, no longer living, I found it a jolt to face a very alive Andy Grove. When he gets to a particularly intense point in a conversation, Grove leans forward and fixes you directly with his eyes, which are a startling blue. "That is not the right question," he will say, briefly taking over the duties of the interviewer. It's not personal. It's about an invisible third party: the truth. The truth is so precious and so hard to coax into view—surrounded by its bodyguard of politics and half-truths—that there is simply no time for fuzzy thinking. There are moments when you can almost experience firsthand the flow of self that went into Intel. And Grove's state of the art memory can transport you from the deck of his home—where a commanding view of Silicon Valley spreads out at his feet—to vivid places in time. Like the day not long after the Stanford case study when Intel executives Craig Kinnie and Dennis Carter arrived in his cubicle to confront him.

In the run-up to the speech about technology choices, Grove had uncharacteristically wavered. He'd told Stanford's Burgelman that he was inclined to stick with Intel's mainstay chip technology known as CISC (for complex instruction set computing don't ask). But when Intel published its annual report, the cover included a new, fashion-forward RISC chip (for reduced instruction set computing). Engineers across the industry were enamored of RISC because of its elegance: It required fewer transistors to accomplish most computing tasks. Grove had even appeared in an Intel rap video to promote RISC.

But Kinnie and Carter had trained at the Grove school of management—Grove's MO as a leader has always been to depend on "helpful Cassandras" to make sure that he doesn't win an argument he ought to lose. The two were blunt. "Andy, you can't do this," Carter said. Abandoning CISC for RISC, they argued, would truncate one of the most profitable franchises in business history for ... what? Leveling the playing field for Intel's competition? When the discussion ended, Kinnie and Carter had achieved a feat of monumental difficulty. They'd won an argument with Andy Grove.

Grove has been grateful to them ever since. He looks back at this episode with anger—at himself. "We almost wrecked the company," he told me. "We had established our technology as the industry standard. This franchise was worth millions, billions. We ... I ... almost walked away from it because the elegance of a new product seduced me into taking my eye off the market." The sun is shining, the view is stunning, and Andy Grove is berating himself for a mistake he didn't make a decade and a half ago. It's a

> "ALMOST WRECKED THE COMPANY BECAUSE A NEW PRODUCT SEDUCED ME."

measure of the demanding life he has lived—a life that, at critical junctures, has hung on Grove's ability to transform himself, to move from role to role as the moment required.

The Early Adapter

To be born a Hungarian Jew in 1936 was to be born on the wrong side of history. Grove was forced to adapt to a succession of threatening realities from the very beginning.

Transformations were the story of Grove's young life. When the Nazis invaded Hungary in 1944, his mother changed his name from Andras Grof to the Slavic Andras Malesevics. When the communists arrived the following year, he once again became Andras Grof. As a young man, he switched from journalism to chemistry after publishers started rejecting his articles for political reasons.

Communism nauseated him. One of his most vivid recollections is the May Day parade of 1950. Cheering was broadcast from loudspeakers around Budapest. But when Andy and his schoolmates arrived at Heroes' Square, they discovered there was no crowd at all: The cheering was recorded. Six years later, when the Hungarian Revolution caused the border with Austria to be open for a brief period, Grove faced an immediate and unanticipated decision. He had never been outside Hungary. An only child, he would be leaving parents he might never see again. He had little idea of what he'd be running to. If ever there was a plunge into the unknown, that was it.

He arrived in the U.S. on Jan. 7, 1957—the same day that

Time's "Man of the Year" issue featured THE HUNGARIAN FREEDOM FIGHTER on its cover. Soon he would change his name for a third and final time. At the City College of New York, where he enrolled, Andras Istvan Grof was struck from the transcript and above it was written Andrew Stephen Grove. He had left behind his home, and he needed a name people could pronounce.

The Self-Made Manager

By the late 1960s Grove had earned a Ph.D. in chemical engineering at the University of California at Berkeley and joined Fairchild Semiconductor, birthplace of the integrated circuit. When colleagues Robert Noyce and Gordon Moore quit to start Intel, Grove declared he was coming too. In 1968 they put their 32-year-old protégé in charge of operations. That forced Grove into an unfamiliar role: having to lead people.

Quite suddenly Grove found himself on the shop floor of a manufacturing startup. There the human dynamics proved far more complex than the fluid dynamics he'd studied at Berkeley. The job, he quickly recognized, required something he knew nothing about: It required management. What was that, anyway? Grove decided he had to figure it out.

On July 4, 1969, he opened a school notebook and pasted in a clipping from a story in *Time* magazine about movie directors. "Vision to Inspire," it read. "Any director must master formidable complexity. He must be adept at sound and camera work, a soother of egos, a cajoler of the artistic talent. A great director has something more: the vision and force to make all these disparate elements fuse into an inspired whole." Above the clipping, Grove wrote with a red pen: "My job description?"

So began the self-education of Andy Grove, manager. It was a quest in which he immersed himself. His classroom would be a remarkable set of journals that he kept for years—and that have never, until now, been revealed. They're a window into the mind of an engineer grappling with the challenge of managing people. How did a company's growth rate, for instance, relate to its employees' ability to grow? In an entry from the early 1970s, Grove noted, "Three groups of people can be identified: (A) don't belong in their jobs in the first place. These are 'defective choices,' nothing to do with growth. (B) These are the previously discussed cases, people who can't grow with their jobs. (C) This is everybody else, including those that have demonstrated all kinds of growth capability before.

"The point is, there is a growth rate at which everybody fails and the whole situation results in a chaos. I feel it is my most important function (as being the highest-level manager who still has a way to judge the impending failure) to identify the maximum growth rate at which this wholesale failure phenomenon begins."

Grove succeeded where others didn't, in part, by approaching management as a discipline unto itself. There's real urgency in his efforts to school himself: He never lost his Hungarian refugee's apprehension of the risk of imminent failure.

The Change Agent

By 1983, when Grove distilled much of his thinking in his book *High Output Management* (still a worthwhile read), he was president of a fast-growing $1.1-billion-a-year corporation, a leading maker of memory chips, whose CEO was Gordon Moore. Could Grove and Moore save the company from an industry that was filled with ferocious competitors?

In many ways change was in Intel's DNA. It was Moore who had famously observed that the number of transistors you could cram onto a chip tended to double every couple of years (later refined to 18 months). What Moore's Law did not and could not predict was that Japanese firms, too, might master this process and turn memory chips into a commodity. That was change of a different order, and not even Intel was prepared for it.

The company's top executives simply could not believe the growing evidence that they were being out-competed in a market they had created. Intel was the memory company, period. Its chips were in many of the best minicomputers and also in the new breed of machine that was then taking off, the personal computer. In the early 1980s profits from other products helped to sustain the delusion that memories were a viable future.

Intel kept denying the cliff ahead until its profits went over the edge, plummeting from $198 million in 1984 to less than $2 million in 1985. It was in the middle of this crisis, when many managers would have obsessed about specifics, that Grove stepped outside himself. He and Moore had been agonizing over their dilemma for weeks, he recounts in Only the *Paranoid Survive*, when something happened: "I looked out the window at the Ferris wheel of the Great America amusement park revolving in the distance when I turned back to Gordon, and I asked, 'If we got kicked out and the board brought in a new CEO, what do you think he would do?' Gordon answered without hesitation, 'He would get us out of memories.' I stared at him, numb, then said, 'Why shouldn't you and I walk out the door, come back, and do it ourselves?'"

The words "I stared at him, numb" suggest that in the crucial moment, Andy ceased to be Andy. Instead he was Dr. Grove the engineer, the teacher, looking down at his own case study. And from this realm of pure reason he could see that Intel's present course had an obvious ending: disaster. It was a cognitive tour de force, yet within moments Andy Grove the executive returned—and was dismayed by what Andy Grove the teacher had concluded. Professors overturn ideas, but they don't upend lives. "To be completely honest about it," Grove wrote, "as I started to discuss the possibility of getting out of the memory-chip business, I had a hard time getting the words out of my mouth without equivocation." One of his managers even persuaded him "to continue R&D for a product that he and I both knew we had no plans to sell." Grove's devotion to reason did not mean that he was a

> "THERE IS A GROWTH RATE AT WHICH EVERYBODY FAILS, [RESULTING] IN A CHAOS."

machine. Far from it. What he found in the end was the will to do what was painful, the will to let go.

"Welcome to the new Intel," Grove said in a speech not long afterward, to rally the troops behind the decision to exit memories. Intel the memory company was dead, he explained, but there was another product on which it could stake its future: the microprocessor. Invented at Intel in 1971, it had spent the 1970s timing traffic lights and helping bacon packers slice their bacon into even strips. Not all that exciting.

But once IBM chose Intel's microprocessor to be the chip at the heart of its PCs, demand began to explode. Even so, the shift from memory chips was brutally hard—in 1986, Intel fired some 8,000 people and lost more than $180 million on $1.3 billion in sales—the only loss the company has ever posted since its early days as a startup.

The Reality Shifter

Grove and Moore had no way of knowing that Intel was on the verge of a remarkable ten-year run. They did know they were betting the company—and that to make the shift they had to risk angering IBM. The $60-billion-a-year giant was not only Intel's biggest customer but also its biggest shareholder—it had bought a large stake in the company to shore up its shaky supplier.

Intel did not set out to dominate the computer industry any more than humans set out to dominate the planet. In both cases the main concern was survival. Humans were so vulnerable to being eaten by larger, faster creatures that their only hope of survival was to control their environment. The "new Intel," too, was subject to forces beyond its control. Grove would later use a graphic that depicted Intel as a castle with the 386 chip in the center. The castle was under siege by rival chipmakers Sun Microsystems, Harris, Motorola, and NEC, not to mention RISC. But in the mid-1980s, before the graphic was ever made, Intel faced a more basic challenge: It was not so much a kingdom as a vassal state. Its dominant customer, IBM, had long insisted that Intel license its microprocessor designs to other chipmakers so that Big Blue could always be certain of a ready supply of chips at a pleasant price.

Grove decided that had to change. "Finally, we had a real winner of a device," Grove says of the 386 chip. But if Intel wanted a more secure future, "we not only had to win, we had to win our way." The 386 marked a genuine milestone of computer engineering. As Microsoft and other software developers figured out how to make full use of the new chip, Grove knew, the PC market would probably grow even hotter. Yet as long as Intel had to share its designs with other chipmakers, it would always face the anonymous and uncertain life of a parts supplier, subject to the whim of a customer 60 times its size.

To become its own kingdom, Grove realized, Intel had to make itself effectively the sole source of microprocessors. Getting IBM to buy the idea posed a challenge—he had no way of knowing how his giant partner would react—but he knew the status quo did not give Intel the freedom it needed to grow. So Intel moved unilaterally: In 1985, when it launched the 386, it declared the technology would not be licensed to other producers. IBM at first did not build 386s into its machines. But as archrival Compaq picked up the chip, IBM came around, cutting a deal with Intel to make some of the 386s it expected to use in its own chip factories. The gamble had paid off. "To insist on our way meant we might lose," Grove says. "But to me, that is better than losing by compromising your advantages away."

The Fallible Human

During Grove's 11-year tenure as CEO, Intel grew at a compound annual growth rate of nearly 30 percent. Together with Microsoft, Intel supplanted IBM as the dominant standard in computing. In 1992, Intel's profits topped $1 billion for the first time—on $5.8 billion of sales. What made such extraordinary growth possible under Grove's leadership was his continuing ability to adapt to shifting realities—but even Mr. Strategic Inflection Point could stumble.

The 386 caught on, and sure enough, Microsoft used it to transform computing—its smash-hit Windows 3.0 operating system, which debuted in 1990, was designed to work on 386-based machines. Grove's breakthrough about changing the rules of the game opened the door to an epiphany about branding and marketing. In 1990 marketing chief Dennis Carter—the same Dennis Carter who had badgered Grove on RISC—came to him with a scheme to launch a large-scale consumer marketing campaign around the slogan "Intel Inside." It is hard to recapture how foreign the concept of branding was at an engineering company like Intel. According to Carter, when he pitched the idea to a roomful of Intel senior executives, "most of them thought it was nuts. But not Andy. He said, 'It's brilliant. Go make it happen.'" Improbably, it turned an internal component into one of the most recognized brands in the world. Grove so loved the idea of marketing to consumers that he selected the name Pentium himself.

There's a rate of growth, though, at which everybody fails, including Andy Grove. His biggest tumble from the learning curve began in 1994. That fall Thomas Nicely, a mathematician at Lynchburg College in Virginia, spotted "inconsistencies" in the way Intel's latest Pentium chip performed a rare, complex scientific calculation.

Intel engineers knew about the bug but deemed it too insignificant to report. By their calculations, a spreadsheet user would encounter it once every 27,000 years of spreadsheet use. But when Nicely's findings were posted on an Internet newsgroup, the discussion became a tempest, then burst into public view. Soon IBM announced it was suspending shipments of its Pentium-based computers.

It was a moment when Grove should have switched into observer mode and asked, "What has changed here?" Instead, he kept thinking like an engineer and waded into the online mob himself, as though it were purely a technical debate. The uproar grew, though, until Grove was forced to adopt a no-questions-asked replacement policy and to apologize to customers. The apology was not very gracious. "What we view as a minor technical problem has taken on a life of its own," he declared. "We apologize. We were motivated by a belief that replacement is simply unnecessary for most people. We still feel that way." In effect he was telling consumers that they wanted something they did not need, but Intel had decided to indulge their irrationality.

A customer replied on the Internet with a poem:

> *When in the future we wish to deride*
> *A CEO whose disastrous pride*
> *Causes spokesmen to lie and sales streams to dry*
> *We'll say he's got Intel Inside.*

For a man who strives to grasp objective reality, Grove had missed a fundamental shift in the nature of his business. Intel had become a marketing company. And while a chip is built in a factory, a brand is co-created with the customer. This required a rethinking of the meaning of "objectivity." In branding, a customer's subjective reality, even if confused, becomes your objective reality. The learning experience was more expensive than most: The Pentium recall required a $475 million write-down that marred Intel's year.

The Data-Driven Patient

A few months later Grove faced crisis again: He was diagnosed with prostate cancer. In the intense period that followed, he remained on the job for all but two-and-a-half days. He handled the decision about his treatment the same way he handled decision-making at Intel: as if life depended on it.

Grove had never been one to rely on others' interpretations of reality. Hungary, in this regard, served as How-Not-To-Do-It University. Reality there was shaped by one's position in the system. At Intel he fostered a culture in which "knowledge power" would trump "position power." Anyone could challenge anyone else's idea, so long as it was about the idea and not the person—and so long as you were ready for the demand "Prove it." That required data. Without data, an idea was only a story—a representation of reality and thus subject to distortion. Hungary had been a grotesque funhouse mirror. The slim man looked fat, and the fat man slim. But when he was diagnosed with prostate cancer in 1995, Grove found himself in the position of most patients: frightened, disoriented, and entirely reliant on the advice of doctors. Their advice was straightforward: Surgery was the best option, and that was pretty much all there was to it.

Was it, though? It took very little to discover that there was much, much more to it. There were alternatives to surgery. No surgeon advised him to take them seriously. But the expert opinions, Grove soon determined, were just that—opinions, based on little if any hard data. Data did exist. What Grove found most shocking is that no one had done the hard work of pulling it together. Plainly, Grove would have to do it himself.

The patient, in effect, became his own doctor. It was a massive research undertaking whose details Grove chronicled in a 1996 story for *Fortune*. One is left with the image of Grove, awake late at night, plotting and cross-plotting the data in his own methodically constructed charts. What did the data tell him? That he would be better off with an alternative procedure known as radiation seeding. That was the treatment he selected.

What Grove found most appalling, in the end, was the utter fixity of belief among doctors who failed to separate knowledge from conventional wisdom. Even the doctor who carried out Grove's procedure was captive to it. "If you had what I have, what would you do?" Grove asked him at one point. The doctor said he'd probably have surgery. Confounded, Grove later asked why. The doctor thought about it.

GROVE'S HARD LESSON ABOUT SELLING TO CONSUMERS COST INTEL $475 MILLION.

"You know," Grove remembers him saying, "all through medical training, they drummed into us that the gold standard for prostate cancer is surgery. I guess that still shapes my thinking."

"Let's Think for Ourselves"

Grove stepped down as CEO in spring 1998 to become Intel's chairman. The betting at Intel was that he'd never really let go of the reins, but Andy surprised everyone. He dug into his new assignment as he has every other—setting out to examine and improve the way the board governed Intel and thereby to set an example for corporate boards everywhere.

In May 2005, when Paul Otellini succeeded Craig Barrett as CEO, Grove officially became "senior advisor" to the company. The title didn't matter. Grove was still teaching.

On a Monday in December 2005, Grove stood before 400 or so Intel employees, the advance troops of the company's health-care initiative. (Intel wants to make its chips the basic building blocks of 21st-century health-care and medical technology.)

Many had never seen Grove in person before, and he got a standing ovation before he said a word. His speech was a strong statement about strategy. Understanding comes from action. So "be quick and dirty," he said. "Engage and then plan. And get it better. Revolutions in our industry in our lifetime have taken place using exactly this formula. The best example is the IBM PC"—created on the fly by a team in Boca Raton.

Then he took questions. A European software engineer stood up with microphone in hand. He asked about handling health-care information. "How can we address the problem of privacy protection and data protection?"

"Stay with me for a minute," Grove said quickly. "Can I ask you a question? Why do you care?"

"Because health-care information might find its way to insurance companies and might result in higher insurance rates," the engineer replied.

"Explain to me why," said Grove, almost before the engineer could finish speaking.

"Many people have said it would be a bad thing if insurers knew all about the health history of everyone in the population," he replied.

Intel's senior advisor sized up the engineer's comments this way: "I think we have a tendency toward adding imaginary complexities to a problem which is already unimaginably complicated." He added, "Let's think for ourselves. Let's not repeat mindlessly ... excuse me, automatically ... suppositions that are true merely because somebody else says they are."

Did the engineer care about having been cross-examined and momentarily called mindless in the presence of 400 coworkers by his legendarily blunt leader? He smiled at Grove's choice of words. "Go ahead," he told Grove. "I was prepared."

RICHARD S. TEDLOW is a historian at the Harvard Business School. His book, *The American: The Life and Times of Andy Grove*, will be published in 2006. For this essay he has drawn on his research, which includes interviews with Grove and many other executives, unpublished documents, and published reports.

Great
TEAMS

V

*Let Leaders Who Break the
Mold Be Your Inspiration*

GREAT TEAMS

How the Best Make It Happen

In 1972 a crack commando unit was sent to prison by a military court for a crime they didn't commit. These four men promptly escaped from a maximum-security stockade to the Los Angeles underground. Today, still wanted by the government, they survive as soldiers of fortune. If you have a problem, if no one else can help, and if you can find them, maybe you can hire the A-Team.

The *A-Team* went off the air in 1987—still wanted by the government—but television has never produced a better blueprint for team-building. The key elements of its effectiveness: a cigar-chomping master of disguise, an ace pilot, a devilishly handsome con man, a mechanic with a mohawk, and an amazingly sweet van. Those particulars might not translate to all business settings. But clear definition of roles is a hallmark of effective collaboration. So is small team size—though four is slightly below the optimal number, 4.6. And the presence of an outside threat—like imminent recapture by government forces—likewise correlates with high team cohesion. To wit: France and England, which bloodied each other for centuries before they noticed ... Germany. Another universal characteristic of teams is that they're, well, universal. If you work for a living, we're guessing you interact with other humans. (Lighthouse keepers, we'll see you next time.)

The fact is, most of what you've read about teamwork is bunk. So here's a place to start: Tear down those treacly motivational posters of rowers rowing and pipers piping. Gather every recorded instance of John Madden calling someone a "team player." Cram it all into a dumpster and light the thing on fire. Then settle in to really think about what it means to be a team.

Teamwork is a practice. We will go further and say: Teamwork is an individual skill. That happens to be the title of a book. Christopher Avery writes, "Becoming skilled at doing more with others may be the single most important thing you can do" to increase your value—

regardless of your level of authority. As work is increasingly broken down into team-sized increments, Avery's argument goes, blaming a "bad team" for one's difficulties is, by definition, a personal failure, since the very notion of teamwork implies a shared responsibility. You can't control other people's behavior, but you can control your own. "Men work together," wrote Robert Frost, "whether they work together or apart." —*BY JERRY USEEM*

FROM WHARTON TO WAR

By Jim Vesterman

Going to war wasn't a textbook career move. In 2002, Jim Vesterman, an Amherst grad who had spent several years in the business world, was scheduled to begin the MBA program at Wharton. For some time, however, he had considered joining the military—both out of a sense duty and because he felt that it would challenge him like nothing in the civilian world could. Then 31, he wondered if this was his last shot. Wharton let him defer admission, so Vesterman set his sights on the elite Marine Corps' Special Ops unit called Force Recon, whose members are drawn from enlisted men rather than the officer ranks. He was able to sign on for two years of active duty and two years in the Reserves, rather than the normal four to six years of active duty. The catch: If he didn't make it into Recon, he was headed for a long tour, starting as a private. Vesterman knew that he'd learn to jump from airplanes and survive behind enemy lines. But he had no idea he'd learn so much about what it meant to be part of a team. He agreed to share his experiences—from his first day at boot camp through his tour in Iraq.

"I CAN'T BREATHE! I can't breathe!" yelled a fellow

Marine Corps recruit during our early boot-camp training in the tear-gas chamber. The drill instructor's response: "I! I! I! What does 'I' have to do with anything?"

From the first day in boot camp, we were told we weren't allowed to use the word "I."

This was completely different from my experience in the business world, where I'd spent the past seven years. Throughout my career "I" had to do with almost everything. Though I considered myself a pretty good team player, personal success and achievement were my real benchmarks. Yet everything I thought I knew about working with other people was about to change. It started on April 22, 2002, the first day of boot camp on Parris Island—when we learned to make our beds.

It's called "two sheets and a blanket." When the drill instructor begins counting, you've got three minutes to make the bed—hospital corners and the proverbial quarter bounce. When you're done, you're told to get back in a line. The goal is to have every bed in the platoon made. So I made my bed, then I stood on the line. I was pretty proud, because when three minutes were up, there weren't more than ten men who had finished. "Ahead of the pack," I thought. But the drill instructors weren't congratulating us. Everyone's bed had to be made. So rip off the sheets and do it again.

I ripped off the sheets, made the bed, and stood on the line. "We've got all day to get this right," the drill instructors were saying, looking at all the unfinished beds. "Two sheets and a blanket!"

I ripped off the sheets again, and again, and again. Finally one of the drill instructors looked me in the eye. "Your bunkmate isn't done. What are you doing?" I thought, "What am I doing?" Standing on line, thinking I'd accomplished something, while my bunkmate struggled.

Together my bunkmate and I made our beds about twice as fast as we did alone. Still, not everyone was finishing. Finally we realized, "Okay, when we're done, we've got to go help the bed next to us, and the bed down from that," and so on. I went from thinking, "I'll hand my bunkmate a pillow, but I'm not going to make the bed for him" to making beds for anyone who needed help. That first lesson was an epiphany for me: You can't survive in the Marine Corps without helping the guy next to you.

After 13 weeks of boot camp, Vesterman graduated first in his platoon of about 50 recruits. He then spent eight weeks at Infantry School, where he passed a Marine Special Ops physical qualifying test called the Recon Indoc, and was sent to RIP (Reconnaissance Indoctrination Platoon), then to Amphibious Reconnaissance School (Recon School), considered one of the most challenging schools in the U.S. military. On average, 40% of those who have already passed all previous screenings will quit Recon School within the first week.

In Recon School, everything gets more intense. Recon Marines are trained to conduct missions behind enemy lines in small teams, usually comprising six men. As the physical and mental challenges get more extreme, you become ever more reliant on your team—both to accomplish missions and simply to survive. We'd go for six or seven days without sleep, and in the middle of some chaotic exercise, the instructor would say, "The guy next to you is down. You get him to that ravine." I'm 5-foot-7, and it took more than I thought I had to put some 230-pound guy on top of the pack on my back and run. Until Recon School, I don't think I ever really let anyone carry my weight. I don't think I was man enough to say, "Hey, I can't do this" or "You're stronger than I am at this. I need help." Then came the telephone pole.

Running five miles while carrying a telephone pole is a grueling task—made more so when it's a race between your six-man team and several others. The only instructions: move our telephone pole along the route, don't let it touch the ground, come in first. "It pays to be a winner," shouted the instructor, a phrase in Recon-speak that let us know there was a reward for coming in first. The race began immediately, so we had to come up with the best technique on the fly. There was no time to discuss a strategy or organize our process. My team strug gled at first, but our approach evolved quickly. We had four guys carrying the pole and two resting by jogging alongside. When we switched off, we decided, it should be the two guys hurting the most-not necessarily the two who had been carrying the longest—who got to rest.

Nobody, especially a type A Recon Marine, wants to be the person who's "not carrying his weight." But some of these guys were simply workhorses—they could run forever with this thing- and some of us could not. We were learning to put team success ahead of our own egos. That was the only way we could move the fastest as a team and win the race. This was a huge change.

Vesterman was the Honor Grad in Recon School—graduating first in his class of around 50 Marines. He went on to complete Airborne Jump School, Marine Combat Dive School, and finally SERE School (Search, Evasion, Resistance, and Escape), where Marines learn to survive as POWs. He was moved to reserve status and two weeks later, in August 2003, began his MBA courses at the Wharton School.

Back in Philadelphia, I quickly became enmeshed in Wharton's own team structure, including my first-year 60-student MBA cohort and my learning team of six peers. In your first year, the majority of projects are done in these peer groups. You're thrown together, graded together, and have to keep up with a flood of assignments, so it's an intense experience. I felt I had made a strong commitment to this new team.

At the end of my first semester, I learned that my unit, 3rd Force Reconnaissance Company, was being called up to serve in Iraq. That same week Peter Pace, vice chairman of the Joint Chiefs (and now chairman), came to Wharton and spoke to my class. When it came around to question time, I raised my hand. "Sir, it looks like I'm being called to serve in Iraq. Do you have any advice for me?" At that point I hadn't even told my classmates yet, and I had very mixed feelings about going to combat and leaving my Wharton team midyear. General Pace, a Marine, didn't reply for three or four seconds. Then he looked at me and the first thing he said was simply, "Congratulations." Immediately, everything became clear to me. The Marine Corps' highest purpose is to serve the nation in time of war, and it was my once-in-a-lifetime opportunity to serve.

The Marine Corps and the Army had entered Iraq in March 2003. Once a war is over it falls to the Army to keep the peace, but when the insurgency surfaced, and then continued, the Marines were sent back in. After several weeks at Camp Pendleton, Calif., in February 2004, Vesterman and his platoon were among the first Marines to be redeployed to the Anbar province in western Iraq.

The youngest guy on our six-man team was 24; the oldest was 38. Our backgrounds ranged from a plant manager to a SWAT cop. Some of us had known each other for a few months, others for nearly a decade. Six totally different lives. But very quickly it felt like we were moving as one—instinctively. We didn't do a lot of speaking. When you need something like binoculars from your pack, you don't stop, put the pack down, and open it, because if you're attacked, the group can't respond immediately. You just say to the guy behind you "I need binos," and you hold security for both of you while he gets them and reseals your pack. When he hits your pack, it means "ready."

There's a tremendous level of trust required between Marines. But since boot camp it's been drilled into all of us to do the right thing. Whether it's good for you or not. Whether it's easy or hard. Whether someone is watching or you're alone.

Our specialty was to enter a town unseen and set up shop there for days at a time in order to do reconnaissance and launch raids. Everyone on a Recon team

> THE ARINES DRILL IT INTO EACH RECRUIT: DO THE RIGHT THING, WHETHER IT'S GOOD FOR YOU OR NOT, WHETHER IT'S EASY OR HARD.

has a different role, but each person needs to be able to move into any job. I learned in the Marine Corps that the strongest teams have members who transition easily between roles. On one mission in a violent town along the border with Syria, we took up a clandestine position in an abandoned building that provided a good view of an intersection where many roadside bombs had been detonated. Our surveillance began to focus on a group of men who were meeting repeatedly on a nearby corner. The man who appeared to be the leader was wearing purple pants, so that's what we called him.

Suddenly we spotted these men retrieving objects in burlap bags from a nearby ravine and moving them in a pushcart toward the corner. They needed to move only 200 meters before they were out of our sights. While we thought the objects were bombs, we weren't sure, so we couldn't engage from our sniper position.

We had only seconds to confer. Then our team leader made the call: "Four men go and intercept." The other two would stay behind and maintain watch from an elevated and defensible position. What followed was the sort of chaotic scene our team was trained for. We exited our position and covered 500 meters at a dead sprint. A local lookout had warned the men, however, and as we turned the corner, the only thing visible was the pushcart.

We instinctively split into buddy teams—you never work alone—and my buddy and I began searching the area while the other team moved toward the pushcart. We recognized one of the men moving away from the scene and intercepted him. While I flex-cuffed the man, my partner moved to hold security.

The same coordination was happening with the other buddy team: One held security while the other opened the abandoned pushcart. As we suspected, there were two Saddam-era artillery shells inside, rigged as bombs. We immediately called this back to our team leader, who was then able to take a shot on "purple pants" when he momentarily reappeared at the original corner. "Purple pants" ended up escaping that day with only a shot to the arm, but we captured him a few weeks later.

We didn't react as six individuals that day. We were one team. Our platoon commander would often quote Kipling to describe the Marines: "The strength of the pack is the wolf, and the strength of the wolf is the pack." The Marine Corps recruits wolves. But its strength comes from training them to fight as a pack.

For his actions that day, Vesterman was awarded the Navy and Marine Corps Achievement Medal. After finishing a seven-month tour, he and his team turned in their gear. Six weeks later, in November 2004, he returned to Wharton.

Elasticity of demand. That's what they talked about in my first class back at Wharton. That culture shock was more jarring than going to Iraq. I slowly came to. In many ways there's probably no better preparation I could have had for the business world than joining the Marine Corps. The Marines teach you how to be both a leader and a follower. I don't have to lead in every situation—but I've come to enjoy stepping up in a time of chaos. When I'm working with a group now, I can honestly say that I think about the team first. The "I first" approach has been drilled out of me.

I'm certainly not the only veteran at Wharton, and for the past several years, the veterans' club has organized a field trip to the Marine Corps Officer Candidate School in Quantico, Va. Students with no military experience are suddenly crawling through mud and under barbed wire while drill instructors shout orders. Two months before I graduated, we made the trip again.

The first drill was familiar: two sheets and a blanket.

LINCOLN'S GENIUS

By Jia Lynn Yang

At the 1860 Republican National Convention, a lawyer with only a single term in Congress to his political credit beat three seasoned politicians for the nomination. Once Abraham Lincoln won the presidency, he asked his rivals to join his administration—a decision at the heart of Doris Kearns Goodwin's book, *Team of Rivals: The Political Genius of Abraham Lincoln.* *Fortune*'s Jia Lynn Yang asked Goodwin how Lincoln did it.

What was Lincoln thinking? Most Presidents in previous decades picked supporters to be in the cabinet. Lincoln takes the opposite approach. He is saying, in effect, "These three rivals are the strongest men in the country. I have no right to deprive it of their services." William Seward, who became Secretary of State, had been a governor and Senator in New York. Salmon Chase, later Lincoln's Treasury Secretary, was governor of Ohio. And Edward Bates, appointed Attorney General, was an accomplished judge. Lincoln thought it was worth having the best talent.

So how did he win them over? Lincoln had such sensitive antennae. He understood how to share credit and how to shoulder blame. He knew how to use humor. We know so much about his management style because of the letters he would write. When he was angry with one of them, he had this tendency of writing what he called a hot letter. Then he would put it aside, waiting for his emotions to cool down, and never send it.

How did Lincoln manage these egos-including his own? That's absolutely the great mystery of Lincoln. He had a deep self-confidence. But on the other hand he didn't allow his short-term ego to get in the way. He always had the larger goal in front of him. He thought, "I can deal with any of these old grudges as long as I feel we are pulling together to accomplish the goal of eventually saving the Union and emancipating the slaves."

BITING THE APPLE

By Ellen McGirt

They were known as dropouts, artists, evangelists, geniuses, iconoclasts, pirates—and friends. Sometimes even best friends. The early team of four, which grew to dozens, wanted to make a personal computer easy enough for a civilian to use without fear or loathing and inexpensive enough to be affordable. But the happy few who worked on the Mac also saw in the new world of computing a potentially profound force. Their ultimate goal was to unleash, in themselves and others, limitless individual creativity.

The Mac team, headed by Apple co-founder Steve Jobs, operated like a superstealth startup within the company. Holed up in an ascetic, two-story building near a gas station dubbed the "Texaco Towers," the team was intensely competitive with other Apple divisions, such as the Lisa computer. Jobs set ridiculous deadlines: The caffeine-fueled software team once debugged for 48 hours straight rather than face him without having finished the task. There were epic battles and broken friendships—Jef Raskin, who started the Mac research project in 1979, got frustrated and left Apple in 1982. But Jobs's famous rebel yell—"It's better to be a pirate than join the Navy"—captured the renegade spirit that saw the team through 90-hour workweeks at stunningly low pay.

In 1983, after three years of labor, the Mac was born. Priced at $2,495, it featured a clean, intuitive graphic user interface that allowed nonprogrammers to use it almost instantly, without geek supervision. When it was turned on, a friendly little icon smiled out at the world. And the world smiled back—the Mac sold faster than any PC that came before. Although the Mac went on to a difficult adolescence, it was the collective expression of the people who loved it—and marked a turning point in the history of the PC.

THIS CAR SAVED FORD

By Ellen McGirt

Call it the $3 billion jellybean. When the Taurus debuted in 1985, its curves and sweeping lines made it different. So was the team that created it. Desperate after losing $1.5 billion in 1980, Ford crushed the status quo—isolated groups that made part of a car to "pass over the wall" to another. Enter Team Taurus. Nearly 400 engineers, designers, and marketers were put in a room and set loose. They brainstormed their way into history-and Ford back into business. Derided at first as the "jellybean" for its shape, the Taurus was *Motor Trend*'s Car of the Year in 1986-and then was imitated. Discontinued in 2005, it enjoys retirement as a corporate fleet fave.

RAZR'S EDGE

By Adam Lashinsky; Research Associate Susan Kaufman

Hundreds of Motorolans jammed into a company auditorium in Schaumburg, Ill., in December 2006 to mourn the sudden death of their storyteller-in-chief. It was a bittersweet moment for Motorola. Geoffrey Frost, the 56-year-old marketing genius responsible for the company's snappy "Hello Moto" ad campaign, had died in his sleep of a heart attack two weeks earlier. Thanks in no small part to Frost's dramatic flair, the proud but humbled company was on the upswing for the first time in years. CEO Ed Zander, who eulogized Frost that day, had promoted him to executive vice president only hours before he died. Frost, you see, had become a symbol of Motorola's resurgence as an unexpectedly stylish technology powerhouse.

For a few engineers and industrial designers attending the memorial service, though, Frost represented something more.

The celebration of his life drew attention to their greatest accomplishment, the creation just two years earlier of the ultra-thin, superhip RAZR V3, the hottest Motorola phone in nearly a decade. Frost had been the phone's cheerleader; he'd come up with its catchy four-letter name. He also had spun an appealing narrative about how Motorola was cool again, and a myth about the slick downtown Chicago design studio where the phone had taken shape.

What the unsung team of heroes knew, however, was that the actual story of how the RAZR came to be is even more compelling than, if not quite as glamorous as, the version Frost had peddled. In reality, the RAZR—a play on a code name the geeks themselves dreamed up—was hatched in colorless cubicles in exurban Libertyville, an hour's drive north of Chicago. It was a skunk-works project whose tight-knit team repeatedly flouted Motorola's own rules for developing new products. They kept the project top-secret, even from their colleagues. They used materials and techniques Motorola had never tried before. After contentious internal battles, they threw out accepted models of what a mobile telephone should look and feel like. In short, the team that created the RAZR broke the mold, and in the process rejuvenated the company.

The mood inside Motorola was grim in early 2003. Nokia,

whose "candy bar" phone designs were all the rage, had snatched Motorola's No. 1 worldwide market share, and wireless operators were decidedly underwhelmed by the models Motorola had to offer. The outlook was equally gloomy for a veteran Motorola engineer named Roger Jellicoe. An Englishman who'd lived in the Chicago area for nearly 20 years, Jellicoe had worked on numerous Motorola phones, including the StarTAC, the company's last monster hit, in 1996. But Jellicoe, 50, who sports a pale-brown salt-and-pepper goatee, had recently had a project yanked out from under him, a high-end phone targeted for overseas markets that had been reassigned to a Motorola design center in Beijing. He was, quite literally, between assignments.

Fortunately for Jellicoe, another project was percolating. Engineers in Motorola's concept-phone unit had mocked up an impossibly thin phone-at ten millimeters, it was half the girth of a typical flip-top-and Rob Shaddock, a senior wireless executive, was casting about for an engineer to lead the team that would commercialize it. Jellicoe aggressively promoted himself for the job and in the spring of 2003 maneuvered a dinner with Shaddock to make his case. They met at Ferkin's, a cheerful pub in downtown Libertyville with better-than-average food and 24 beers on tap. In advance Jellicoe had drawn up sketches of what the phone might look like (drawings that bear a striking resemblance to the RAZR today). Midway through the meal, Shaddock told Jellicoe the job was his.

Jellicoe's instructions were to create the thinnest phone ever released-and to do it within a year. The goal was to make a splash at the next year's Academy Awards, on the last day of February 2004. Celebrities would be seen clutching these new prizes, and publicity would rain down on the company. The phone was supposed to be something beautiful, like jewelry-a pricey gem in the $500 range at retail, rather than a mass-market staple. Motorola needed a reputation builder, badly. The moneymaker phones would come after, or so the plan went, piggybacking on the company's restored allure.

For a Motorola lifer like Jellicoe, this task, while daunting, was also liberating. If the phone was never meant to be a blockbuster-if it was in essence a high-end toy, judged on its wow factor more than its sales-that gave him license to take some chances.

To design the innards of a telephone takes a team of specialists. Jellicoe, an electrical engineer, turned to an old pal, Gary Weiss, a mechanical engineer with whom Jellicoe had once designed a phone over a cup of coffee at Starbucks. The project's appeal proved to be a talent magnet within the company, and the two quickly assembled a team that grew to as many as 20 engineers. The full group met daily at 4 p.m. in a conference room in Libertyville to hash over the previous day's progress as they worked down a checklist of components: antenna, speaker, keypad, camera, display, light source, and so on. Scheduled for an hour, the meetings frequently ran past 7 p.m.

The "thin clam" project became a rebel outpost. Money wasn't an object, but secrecy and speed were. Normally Motorola consults closely with the wireless companies that sell the phones to try to integrate whatever

> THE GOAL WAS AN
> *IMPOSSIBLY THIN PHONE*
> AT TEN MILLIMETERS—
> AND IT HAD TO BE
> BEAUTIFUL AS A JEWEL.

favorite features they request. It also conducts "mall intercepts" to gauge consumers' reaction. Not this time. Jellicoe hid the details of the project even from company colleagues. "Anytime you've got something radically different, there will be people who feel that we should be putting our resources on other stuff," he says. For cover, Jellicoe relied on Shaddock, who says, "It was a kind of lock-the-door-and-put-the-key-beneath-it approach to product development." Digital pictures of the project were prohibited, so nothing could be inadvertently disseminated by e-mail. Models of the phone could leave the premises only when physically accompanied by a team member.

As Jellicoe's engineers focused on the inside of the slender phone, a soft-spoken industrial designer named Chris Arnholt was envisioning what it would look like on the outside. Arnholt, 30 at the time, had joined Motorola two years before from a design boutique in Rochester, N.Y., called KEK. Ponytailed and usually dressed all in black, Arnholt carries two checkbook-sized notebooks, one for writing down things to do, the other for observations he doesn't want to forget. "Design is really about communication," he says. "Sometimes my ideas are tough to communicate." Arnholt was the yin to the engineers' yang. Where they calculated radio frequencies, he pondered the curve of the phone's "knuckles," or hinges. While they bounced around one another's workstations at the office, Arnholt escaped to his tranquil apartment in Highland Park, a lakefront suburb near Libertyville, where deer sometimes wandered into the backyard from a nearby forest.

JELLICOE *HID THE DETAILS* OF THE THIN-CLAM PROJECT, EVEN FROM HIS COLLEAGUES WITHIN MOTOROLA.

The phone that became the RAZR owes many of its most distinctive elements—from its smooth aluminum finish to its backlighted keypad—to Arnholt's obsession with what he called "rich minimalism." To conceptualize his design ideas, he'd bring home prototypes made from sculpted cornstarch, and then fashion and refashion their appearance, using masking tape to adjust previous versions. "Chris is excellent at working the details and then refining the hell out of them," says Jim Wicks, Motorola's chief designer. Arnholt would then render his designs onto the page. Another designer would translate them into three-dimensional computer graphics. And from that program, model makers in Libertyville would craft a plastic mockup of the design.

Applying the laws of physics to Arnholt's stylish sketches was an exercise in collaboration, and not always a seamless one.

Through the late summer and early fall of 2003, the engineering and design teams began combining their work, a back-and-forth process that mechanical engineering chief Gary Weiss aptly calls the "dance." Arnholt began attending the daily 4 p.m. meeting, as each roadblock thrown up by the engineers was translated into an endlessly tweaked design. As the team contemplated each feature of the phone, every decision had a snowball effect on another feature. An antenna in one place meant an earphone connector had to go someplace else. The team members—and often their bosses—repeatedly haggled about what the phone should and shouldn't have in it.

Nearly every argument came down to the tradeoff of functionality vs. thinness. Shaddock, for instance, was willing to jettison the caller-ID display on the outside of the flip phone, believing it added unnecessary thickness. Jellicoe felt otherwise: All other high-end phones had that feature. But what might have to go to make room for it?

Two key innovations allowed the team to make quantum leaps in thinness. The first was a Jellicoe brainstorm: placing the antenna in the mouthpiece of the phone instead of at the top. An innovative idea, it was also a technical challenge. Jellicoe set up a competition among five of his engineers to see who could come up with the best design. Tadd Scarpelli, a then-32-year-old engineer who likes to take apart and rebuild car engines in his free time, devised the most elegant solution. The second brainstorm was rearranging the phone's innards, primarily by placing the battery next to the circuit board, or internal computer, rather than beneath it. That solution, however, created a new problem: width. Motorola's "human factors" outfit had concluded that a phone wider than 49 millimeters wouldn't fit well in a person's hand. The side-by-side design yielded a phone 53 millimeters wide.

But the RAZR team didn't accept the company's research as gospel. The team made its own model to see how a 53-millimeter phone felt. Says Frank Stone, a mechanical engineer who worked on the battery placement: "People could hold it in their hands and say, 'Yeah, it doesn't feel like a brick.'" "In the end, the team members decided for themselves that the company was wrong and that four extra millimeters was acceptable. They ended up reaching a similar conclusion about the ten-millimeter-thickness target: Ultimately, they were able to construct a phone with all the features they wanted that measured 13.9 millimeters at the beam, exceeding the target by a little more than an eighth of an inch. Still, that was 40 percent thinner than Motorola's slimmest flip-top phones. Everyone agreed it was more than thin enough for the statement Motorola was trying make.

As the thin-clam team made progress in combative isolation, the mood at Motorola had gone from bad to worse. In the fall of 2003, the company lacked enough camera lenses to supply phones for the coming holiday shopping season. The stock plunged 5 percent in September when word came out about the camera-phone snafu. That same month the board asked CEO Christopher Galvin, a grandson of the company's founder, to retire. In December it further humiliated senior management by hiring an outsider, former Sun Microsystems president Ed Zander, to run the company. Zander started at Motorola on the first business day of 2004 without unveiling a strategy but promising to rid the company of its hidebound ways. He didn't let on publicly, but early in his tenure he got a look at the ultra-thin phone. He liked what he saw.

He wasn't the only Motorolan beginning to sense that this trim phone was something special. Tom Lynch, head of the cellphone division at the time, recalls Rob Shaddock becoming obsessed with it. "Every time I saw him he had it in his hand, whether it was in a staff meeting or having a beer," says Lynch, who has since left Motorola to become CEO of Tyco's electronics business. "He was constantly flipping it open and turning it around and rubbing it."

The phone team did have its troubles. It became clear, for instance, that it would miss the February 2004 deadline. Perfecting the materials and appearance of the cool-blue "night signature" of the keypad was such a sticking point that Chris Arnholt traveled to South Korea to work with the supplier chosen to make keypads for the phone. An Oscar debut would have to wait.

By the summer, almost a year after Arnholt had begun playing with prototypes at his apartment, the phone was ready for its close-up. The thin clam had acquired a formal code name early on. Jellicoe wanted to call it the Siliqua Patula, which is Latin for "razor clam." That bit of geek humor was too much for the team's project manager, Bill Kastritis, who insisted on calling it the Razor, as in razor thin. The initial marketing plan labeled the phone the V3, in keeping with Motorola's naming convention. (Previous phones were the V300, V500, and V600.) Enter Geoffrey Frost, the marketing chief who had paid close attention as the phone project progressed. He was enamored with what the phone could do for Motorola but couldn't bear the thought of such an elegant device going out into the world with such a pedestrian name. Borrowing from the team's code word, he hit on an eye-catcher: the four-letter RAZR.

Lessons from MOTO

1. **Secrecy limits distractions.**
   By insulating its RAZR development team from the influence of corporate group think, Motorola got an innovative product that wowed the industry and consumers.

2. **Research isn't everything.**
   Motorola's "human factors" unit dictated that phones more than 49 millimeters wide would be deemed uncomfortable by consumers. The RAZR team concluded otherwise. Their only data points: their own instincts.

3. **Niche products can have mass appeal.**
   The RAZR wasn't designed to be a blockbuster. It was supposed to be a high-priced, high-end jewel to regain luster for Motorola. Yet with high demand, unit costs plunged along with the price for consumers—to as low as $99.

4. **Missing deadlines doesn't mean failure.**
   The RAZR team was supposed to be done by February 2004; they weren't until summer. But getting it right meant a whole lot more than getting it done on time.

Frost also orchestrated the phone's first public appearance. Motorola had privately shown models to a handful of network executives in backroom presentations at trade shows early in 2004. But in June, Frost's team started feeding the hype machine by offering a sneak peak at a gadget fashion show for design-oriented journalists at Copenhagen's Arken Museum of Modern Art. As for the official unveiling, it is industry tradition that new phones are released at a wireless conference. Zander insisted that, once again, the plan be different for the RAZR. Inspired by the attention Steve Jobs gets each time he debuts a new toy, Zander launched the RAZR in a splashy presentation at Motorola's annual meeting with financial analysts in Chicago in July.

The new phone was a hit, shipping first in Asia and then with Cingular Wireless in the U.S. Yet even at that stage it was positioned as a niche product. In the fourth quarter of 2004, out of the 29 million handsets Motorola shipped, RAZR accounted for an impressive though hardly astronomical 750,000. It was a new executive, Ron Garriques, who took over the cellphone division that September, who pushed for Motorola to go large with the RAZR. "I looked at the budget for 2005, and we were planning two million," recalls Garriques, who previously had been head of European operations. "I said, 'We need to build 20 million.'" How right he was. The company sold even more RAZRs than that in 2005, and projects it will sell its 50-millionth RAZR in June of 2006. "That's one-tenth the time it took the StarTAC to get to that level," notes Garriques. Zander favors a different comparison: "We'll sell more RAZRs in 2006 than Apple will iPods."

In July 2005 several key players from the RAZR development team were asked to appear at a meeting of top executives at company headquarters. They weren't told why. "Even when we were sitting in the room waiting to be called in, nobody was really quite sure what was going to happen," says Tadd Scarpelli, the young engineer who designed the RAZR's antenna. Then, as the team members filed in, the executives awaiting them rose in applause, delivering a standing ovation—followed by news that the team members would also be rewarded with a boatload of stock options. "It was surreal," says Scarpelli, who to this day approaches strangers in airports and asks them if they like "his" phone. Successful rule breakers, after all, have certain privileges.

WHY DREAM TEAMS FAIL

By Geoffrey Colvin

In what universe is it even conceivable that the United States could fail to reach the semifinals of something called the World Baseball Classic? Not only fail to win, but could field a team that included Roger Clemens, Derek Jeter, Alex Rodriguez, and Johnny Damon and then lose games to Mexico, South Korea, and—wait for it—Canada? Yet it happened in 2006.

How could a movie starring Brad Pitt, George Clooney, Catherine Zeta-Jones, and Julia Roberts, directed by Steven Soderbergh, get tepid reviews and gross less worldwide than the star-free *My Big Fat Greek Wedding*? That movie was *Ocean's Twelve*.

And how could a Fortune 500 company run by a brilliant former McKinsey consultant, paying fat salaries to graduates of America's elite business schools, dissolve into fraud and bankruptcy? It happened at Enron. If someone tells you you're being recruited onto a dream team, maybe you should run. In our team-obsessed age, the concept of the dream team has become irresistible. But it's brutally clear that they often blow up. Why? Because they're not teams. They're just bunches of people.

A look at why so many dream teams fail, and why so many of the most successful teams consist of individuals you've never heard of, yields insight into the essential nature of winning organizations. As always when the subject is the real-world behavior of human beings, the takeaway includes things we always knew—even though we rarely behave as if we do.

The most important lesson about team performance is that the basic theory of the dream team is wrong. You cannot assemble a group of stars and then sit back to watch them conquer the world. You can't even count on them to avoid embarrassment. The 2004 U.S. Olympic basketball team consisted entirely of NBA stars; it finished third and lost to Lithuania.

By contrast, the 1980 hockey team that beat the Soviets at the Lake Placid Olympics was built explicitly on anti-dream-team principles. Coach Herb Brooks, who died in 2003, based his picks on personal chemistry. In the story's movie version, *Miracle*, Brooks's assistant looks at the roster and objects that many of the country's greatest college players were left out (professionals were not eligible to play then). To which Brooks responds with this essential anti-dream-team philosophy: "I'm not lookin' for the best players, Craig. I'm lookin' for the right players."

To see why dream teams so often disappoint, let's consider the most common paths to failure.

Signing too many all-stars. "Some of the worst teams I've ever seen have been those where everybody was a potential CEO," says David Nadler, chief of the Mercer Delta consulting firm, who has worked with executive teams at top global companies for more than 30 years. "If there's a zero-sum game called succession going on, it's very difficult to have an effective team."

Chemistry and culture are key. Henry Ford II successfully brought in the Whiz Kids, a pre-assembled team of U.S. Army managerial stars that included Tex Thornton, Robert McNamara, and others, when he sensed that Ford needed a revolution after World War II. Young and iconoclastic, they had a record of working together effectively, and they did well at Ford, helping it to cash in on the postwar boom. But 50 years later when CEO

> "I'M NOT LOOKING FOR THE BEST PLAYERS," SAID THE U.S. HOCKEY COACH. "I'M LOOKIN' FOR THE RIGHT PLAYERS."

Jacques Nasser correctly decided that Ford needed another revolution, he stuck with the old-guard team already in place. Like most old guards, they weren't ready for a real revolution, and when push came to shove, Nasser got ejected. More seriously for Ford, the revolution didn't happen.

For a notably successful method of choosing team members, look at Worthington Industries, the Ohio-based steel processor. When an employee is hired to join a plant-floor team, he works for a 90-day probationary period, after which the team votes to determine whether he can stay. The system works because much of the team's pay is based on performance, so members are clear-eyed and unsparing in evaluating a new candidate's contribution. Worthington's CEO, John McConnell, could be talking about teams at any level when he says, "Give us people who are dedicated to making the team work, as opposed to a bunch of talented people with big egos, and we'll win every time."

That's the philosophy that powers teams such as basketball's Detroit Pistons and especially football's New England Patriots. The Pats have won three Super Bowls in the past five years with few stars and a quarterback, Tom Brady, who was the 199th pick. The Washington Redskins, by contrast, have bought star after star—and floundered.

Failing to build a culture of trust. Read the extensive literature on team effectiveness, or talk to people on teams in sports, business, or elsewhere, and it always comes down to this: Trust is the most fundamental element of a winning team. If people think their teammates are lying, withholding information, plotting to knife them, or just incompetent, nothing valuable will get done. The team doesn't create synergy. It creates "dysergy"—two plus two equals three, with luck.

So dream teams are in trouble right from the start because team members may have particular reasons to be distrustful. In sports settings they are often brought together only briefly from teams that spend the rest of the year trying to beat each other. Even if team members can set aside that antagonistic mind-set, they rarely have time to develop confidence in one another's behavior. It's similar in business: Even if team members aren't battling for the next promotion, someone is always getting moved or stolen away. "A major problem is that people are transient," says consultant Ram Charan. Especially on an all-star team, "there's all the headhunting, and there's a constant tug to have people pulled out of the team. Instability is a major issue." That's a big problem because trust, by its nature, builds slowly.

Many companies try to speed the trust-building process. In the '80s there was a virtual epidemic, often in woodsy corporate off-sites, of people falling backward off tables into the arms of co-workers as a way of learning trust. Maybe it even helped. Today consultants have developed many additional exercises that involve people sharing personal stories or revealing their personality type, based on the valid insight that reciprocal vulnerability is the beginning of trust. But the process can be rushed only so much.

In fact, trust is so fragile and so laboriously created that it may never extend very far in a top-level team. "Building a really high-performing executive team at the highest level is a mirage," says a management consultant who doesn't want to be quoted because this particular message is a downer. "When such teams do exist, they'll consist mostly of two people, maybe three." It's just too hard to build trust more extensively at the top level, where everyone is supposedly a star.

And sure enough, the legendary top executive teams are almost always pairs. Think of Roberto Goizueta and Donald

Keough at Coca-Cola in the '80s and '90s, or Tom Murphy and Dan Burke at Capital Cities/ABC from the '60s to the '90s, or Reuben Mark and Bill Shanahan at Colgate-Palmolive for two decades until last year, or Warren Buffett and Charlie Munger at Berkshire Hathaway from the '60s to today. No one would have called those pairs dream teams back when they got together; at the time, most people had never heard of them.

Maybe you noticed something else about those teams: Each consisted of a boss who became famous and a much less famous No. 2 who devoted his career to the success of the enterprise. In every case, though, they developed deep trust over many years and produced outstanding results.

Tolerating competing agendas. You don't often find examples of the best and worst executive teams involving the same person, but consider the case of Michael Eisner. For the first ten years of his reign at Disney, he and COO Frank Wells formed one of corporate America's great teams. On their watch, Disney revived its glorious animation tradition, and the movie business flourished. Eisner and Wells could take credit for saving a storied company—and making shareholders rich. This productive partnership ended suddenly and terribly when Wells died in a 1994 helicopter crash.

Eisner then formed one of the most famously disastrous teams in recent history, bringing in über-agent Michael Ovitz as president. He lasted only 14 months. In the

Good Teams

George Huntington Hartford and George Gilman In 1859 they founded what became A&P, the first modern supermarket chain. Buying directly from the ships that came into New York, they created a new business model for selling groceries.

William S. Paley owned it; *Frank Stanton* (president, 1946-71) ran it, and from the late 1950s to the mid-'70s, CBS dominated prime time, becoming known as the Tiffany network.

Bernie Marcus and Arthur Blank Fired in 1978 from Handy Dan, a small home-improvement chain, they went on to pioneer the big-box specialty store. Home Depot is now America's No. 2 retailer (behind Wal-Mart), with almost $82 billion in sales.

extensive postmortems, the overriding theme is of conflicting business and personal agendas. Ovitz wanted to buy a major stake in Yahoo, expand Disney's book and record businesses, and buy an NFL franchise, among other big ideas that Eisner dismissed as off-strategy. Ovitz also seemed to have notions of his own future—he spent $2 million remodeling his office-that did not sit well with Eisner. Bottom line: team failure, at tremendous cost to Disney in both money and prestige.

It is many a father's dream to team up with his sons, but family businesses can find it particularly difficult to unpick the personal from the corporate. That is one part of the dynamic that operated at Adelphia, the cable company founded by John Rigas. Even after it went public, Rigas and his sons operated it as if were still a family concern-for example, paying for private expenses from corporate funds. They got nailed, and Adelphia went bankrupt in 2002.

The challenge is to keep the inevitable personal agendas from becoming destructive. That's part of the leader's job. For example, Ameritech in the '90s had an all-star team of top executives that included Richard Notebaert, future CEO of Ameritech, Tellabs, and Qwest, and Richard Brown, future CEO of Cable & Wireless and EDS. Michigan business school professor Noel Tichy, who was advising the company on leadership development at the time, recalls that CEO Bill Weiss told the team bluntly every week that if he caught anybody trying to undermine the others, the guilty party would be fired. It worked.

Letting conflicts fester. Col. Stas Preczewski, coach of the Army crew at West Point a few years ago, faced a baffling problem. Through extensive testing, he had developed objective criteria to rank his rowers. He then put the eight best-his dream team-in the varsity boat and the eight others in the junior varsity boat. The problem: The JV beat the varsity two-thirds of the time. The situation, as explained in a Harvard Business School case, was that the varsity was full of resentment over who was contributing most, while the JV, feeling they had nothing to lose, supported one another happily.

One day Preczewski lined up the varsity crew in four pairs. He told them they were to wrestle—no punching—for 90 seconds. There were no clear winners: Each man was discovering that his opponent was just as strong and determined as he was. Preczewski then had them change opponents and wrestle again. By the third round they were choosing their own opponents— "One guy would point at another and say, 'You!'" Preczewski says. Finally, one of the rowers started laughing, and they all piled into a general brawl. Eventually someone said, "Coach, can we go row now?" From then on, the varsity boat flew.

You probably can't order members of an executive team to wrestle, tempting though it may be. But bringing tensions out into the open and then resolving them is one of the team leader's most important jobs.

Hiding from the real issues. "Put the fish on the table," says George Kohlrieser, a professor at the International Institute for Management Development in Switzerland. You've got to go through the "smelly, bloody process of cleaning it," but the reward is "a great fish dinner at the end of the day." Most people don't want to be the one who puts the proverbial fish on the table. "There's a veneer of politeness," says consultant David Nadler, "or unspoken reciprocity—we won't raise our differences

Bad Teams

*John Rigas, Timothy Rigas, Michael Rigas
The paterfamilias, John, and his sons borrowed huge sums for personal use. Adelphia went into bankruptcy in 2002 after disclosing billions in debt. Much of the Rigas clan ended up in court.

*CEO Phil Condit (1996-2003) and his Boeing brain trust
Dogged by scandal, falling earnings, and the challenge of Airbus, America's premier airplane manufacturer just couldn't fly right.

*Al Dunlap and anyone "Chainsaw Al" liked to portray himself as a tough-minded savior of dying companies (Lily Tulip, Scott Paper, Sunbeam). But the big-talking bully got tossed from Sunbeam and ended up as a symbol of capitalism at its worst.

in front of the boss." Consultant Ram Charan describes a $12 billion division of ABB that was headed for bankruptcy, in part because of "its culture of polite restraint. People didn't express their honest feelings" about the most important issues. The unit's leader turned it around by insisting that team members say what was on their minds.

Jack Welch was one of the great champions of putting the fish on the table—facing reality, as he says. GE's dream team was and is the Corporate Executive Council, which used to meet at headquarters in a formal atmosphere with rehearsed presentations and little real discussion. Welch moved the meetings off-site, forbade prepared presentations and jackets and ties, and lengthened the coffee breaks to encourage informal discussion, among other changes. At GE they call this "social architecture" and believe it was a critical element of Welch's success.

In business, dream teams are usually part of some rescue fantasy, not the real world. "Be prepared to have an imperfect set," says Charan. "Then you've got to devote your energy to getting them to synchronize. It's very time consuming. It taxes your patience." It's life.

To avoid seducing yourself into thinking all your problems might be vaporized by assembling a dream team, resolve now to accept this fact: There was only one Dream Team, and that was the 1992 U.S. Olympic basketball team. Michael Jordan, Magic Johnson, Larry Bird, Charles Barkley, Patrick Ewing—it was a one-time event. (And remember, Bird and Magic, the veteran co-captains, both had reputations as team players.) For the rest of us, putting together a few talented people who will work honestly and rigorously for something greater than themselves—that's more than enough of a dream.

> WHY DO DREAM TEAMS BLOW UP SO OFTEN? BECAUSE THEY'RE NOT TEAMS, JUST BUNCHES OF PEOPLE.

Great
ADVICE

*Words That Define Leadership
to the World's Best Managers*

GREAT ADVICE

Words That Define Leadership to the World's Best Managers

M anagement genius Peter Drucker, who died on Nov. 11, 2005, at age 95, didn't admire "leadership" per se, remarking to *Fortune*, "The three greatest leaders of the 20th century were Hitler, Stalin, and Mao. If that's leadership, I want no part of it." But he had no problem telling you what it took to become a great manager. Below are edited excerpts from Drucker's article "The Effective Executive," followed by advice and opinions on stellar management from today's foremost practitioners.

— Build on People's Strengths —
It is a characteristic of an effective executive that he builds on the strengths of his colleagues. To demand only well-rounded people, people who have only strengths and no weaknesses (whether the term used is the "whole man," the "mature personality," the "well-adjusted personality," or the "generalist"), is to invite mediocrity—of which there is always an abundant supply. There is far too little strength around for us to waste it.

— Know Your Market —
Effective executives make sure they go outside their own business to look, to listen, and to see for themselves. Recently a manufacturer of medical supplies found that it had slipped from a No. 1 position in its field to a poor second. "We have the same products," they told me. "In fact, ours tend to be superior technically." It turned out that the brash competitor had something else. Its top people had made it a point to spend many months a year away from their own organization—in hospitals, in doctor's offices, in operating rooms. They didn't go there to sell. They went there to observe and to listen. As a result they knew what the hospitals needed and in what form; medical men came to look on this company as the natural place to take their ideas.

— Control Your Time —

Certainly there is no such thing as an "effective type." Among the effective executives I have known, there are extroverts and aloof men, some even morbidly shy. Some are eccentrics, others painfully correct conformists. Some are fat and some are lean. Some drink quite heavily, others are total abstainers. Some are men of great charm and warmth, some have no more personality than a frozen mackerel. Yet it is also my observation that effective executives do have in common certain practices or habits—and practices can be learned. One obvious practice is the conservation of time. In a peculiar way the executive's time is everybody else's time but his own. Everybody can move in on him, and usually everybody does. He cannot shut himself off from these demands, but he must use the little time he can control to do the important things. This is the secret of those few people who accomplish so much with so little apparent effort. They put first things first.

— Pull the Weeds —

The problem is not just to get rid of programs and products that have obviously failed. The problem is to get rid of yesterday's successes that have outlived their potential. The effective executive periodically asks, "If we were not already doing this, would we go into it now?" Unless the answer is an unconditional yes, the chances are the activity should be dropped or sharply curtailed. The pressures are usually all the other way. It will be said in effect that "this product built the company, and it's our duty to maintain it and commit more resources." Most executives have learned that what one postpones one actually abandons. As a rule there is nothing less desirable than to take up a project today that one should have initiated yesterday. The timing is almost bound to be wrong, and timing is crucial in any effort. To do five years later what it would have been smart to do five years earlier is almost a sure recipe for frustration and failure.

THE BEST ADVICE I EVER GOT

Interviewers: Julia Boorstin; Cora Daniels; Robert Friedman; Marc Gunther; David Kirkpatrick; Clifton Leaf; Devin Leonard; Carol Loomis; Betsy Morris; David Rynecki; Julie Schlosser; Patricia Sellers; Jerry Useem

Warren Buffett

CEO of Berkshire Hathaway

You're right not because others agree with you, but because your facts are right.

"I had two mentors: my dad, Howard Buffett, and Ben Graham. Here were these two guys who I revered and who over the years gave me tons of good advice. But when I think about what they said to me, the truth is, the first thing that comes to mind is bad advice.

"I was not quite 21 when this happened, in 1951, and just getting out of business school at Columbia. I had just taken Ben's class there— and I was the most interested student you ever saw. I wanted to work for Ben at Graham-Newman Corp., and I had famously gone to him and offered to work for nothing. He said no.

"But I still was determined to go into the securities business, and that's where Ben and my dad gave me the bad advice. They both thought it was a bad time to start. One thing on their minds was that the Dow Jones industrials had been above 200 all year, and yet there had never been a year when it didn't sell below 200. So they both said, 'You'll do fine, but this is not a good time to start.'

"Now there's one thing that may have influenced my dad, and maybe Ben too. I was so immature. I was not only young-looking, I was young-acting. I was skinny. My hair looked awful. Maybe their advice was their polite way of saying that before I started selling stocks, I needed to mature a little, or I wasn't going to be successful. But they didn't say that to me; they said the other. Anyway, I didn't pay any attention. I went back to Omaha and started selling securities at my dad's firm, Buffett Falk.

"My dad was a totally independent thinker. I suppose the fact that he was has influenced my own thinking some when it comes to buying stocks. Ben instructed me some there too. He said, 'You're neither right nor wrong because others agree with you. You're right because your facts and reasoning are right.'

"Now, Ben—I started learning from him when I read his books on investing at the University of Nebraska. I had tried all kinds of investing up to then, but what he said, particularly in *The Intelligent Investor*, just lifted the scales from my eyes-things like 'margin of safety' and how to use 'Mr. Market' rather than letting him use you. I then went to Columbia just to take his class and later got that turndown when I asked him for a job. But I kept thinking about that idea when I went back to Omaha. I kept trying to sell Ben stocks and pestering him, sort of. And finally one day in 1954 I got a letter from him saying something to the effect of the next time you're in New York, I'd like to talk to you about something. I was elated! And I made a point of getting to New York immediately.

"I went to work for Ben in August 1954, without ever having asked what my salary would be. It turned out to be $12,000, plus the next year I got a $2,000 bonus. I worked for both parts of the business: Graham-Newman was a regulated investment company, and Newman & Graham Ltd. was what we'd today call a hedge fund. But together they ran only $12 million!

"Walter Schloss and I—though he left before long to start a hedge fund—worked together in a little room. We had a lot of fun with each other, plus we kept poring through the manuals, looking for cheap stocks. We never went out to visit any companies. Ben thought that would be cheating. And when we found something terrific, Ben would put 50,000 bucks into it.

"By early 1956, Ben was planning to leave the firm to go to

California. And I had already decided by then to go back to Omaha. I had a terrible time telling Ben about that: I'd go into his office and come back, and then go in and not do it, for a really long time. But his reaction was kind of the same as my dad would have had: whatever's best for you.

"I had $9,800 at the end of 1950, and by 1956 I had $150,000. I figured with that I could live like a king. And I didn't know what I was going to do in Omaha. Maybe go to law school. I did not have a plan. I certainly didn't know I was going to start an investing partnership. But then a couple of months later, seven people wanted me to invest their money for them, and a partnership was the way to do it. And that began it all."

Richard Branson
Founder of Virgin Atlantic Airways and the Virgin Group

Make a fool of yourself. Otherwise you won't survive.

"The person who had the biggest impact on me was Freddie Laker. He had been an aviator involved in the Berlin airlift and had made his money flying goods into Berlin at the end of World War II. He started a low-cost airline [Laker Airways, in 1966] that flew over the Atlantic. He was forced out of business by British Airways. I don't know whether I would have gone into the airline business without seeing what happened to him. He was a very charismatic figure. He was taking on the big guys. He would fly his own planes. He created a lot of excitement."At the time, I was running a little record company; I was about 17 years old. The first time I met him was some years later. I was thinking about setting up my own airline. He gave me this advice: 'You'll never have the advertising power to outspend British Airways. You are going to have to get out there and use yourself. Make a fool of yourself. Otherwise you won't survive.'

"The other advice he gave me: 'They [British Airways] will use every trick in the book [against you]. When that happens, three words matter. Only three words, and you've got to use them: Sue the bastards!'

"I suspect if I hadn't sued British Airways [in 1992], Virgin Atlantic wouldn't have survived. And if I hadn't used myself to advertise the airline, then it also wouldn't have survived.

> *"If I hadn't used myself to advertise, we wouldn't have survived."*
>
> —RICHARD BRANSON

"I named one of my airplanes after him: the *Sir Freddie*."

Howard Schultz
Chairman of Starbucks

Recognize the skills and traits you don't possess, and hire people who have them.

"Warren Bennis is one of the most respected scholars on leadership. And I was under a lucky star one day—I heard Warren speak at an event, and I was so impressed by what he said that I sought him out for advice. This was in the late 1980s, long before we were a public company.

"Over the years, Warren has been a valued advisor and mentor, and he has become a trusted friend. It's hard to pinpoint just one piece of advice that he gave me, because his guidance was valuable on so many levels. Early on, I remember his words—he said this many times—that I needed to invest ahead of the growth curve and think beyond the status quo in terms of the skill base, the experience, and the quality of the people around me. He also told me that the art of becoming a great leader is in developing your ability to leave your own ego at the door and to recognize the skills and traits you don't possess and that you need to build a world-class organization.

"This was harder than it sounds, because I wanted to build a different kind of company—a company that had a conscience. So it wasn't only that I needed people with skills and discipline and business acumen that complemented my own qualities, but, most important, I needed to attract and retain people with like-minded values. What tied us together was not our respective disciplines, and it was not chasing an exit strategy driven by money. What tied us together was the dream of building a company that would achieve the fragile balance of profitability, shareholder value, a sense of benevolence, and a social conscience."

A.G. Lafley
Chairman and CEO of Procter & Gamble

Have the courage to stick with a tough job.

"My mom, a strong, proud Irish woman who died last year at 82, told me to have the courage of my convictions. She encouraged me to be independent and to be myself, and her advice was in my mind when I almost left P&G in my sixth year. It was 1982, and I decided to go to one of those boutique consulting firms in Connecticut. I even bought a house in Connecticut. I was getting out of P&G because I thought the bureaucracy was so stifling and the change was so slow. I was an associate-between a brand manager and a marketing director—and I was running a bunch of laundry brands. Steve Donovan was in charge of the soap business, and I handed him my resignation.

"He tore it up. I said to him, 'I made a copy.' He said, 'Go home. Call me tonight.' Which was smart, not to negotiate with me right there. When I called him that night, he said, 'Don't come into the office for the next week. Come and see me every night.' So every night, I went to his home, and we'd have a beer or two. He kept working me over until he got to the root of my problem with P&G, which was the bureaucracy. He said, 'You're running away. You don't have the guts to stay and change it. You'll run from the next job too.'

> *"He said, 'You're running away. You don't have the guts to stay.'"*
> —A.G. Lafley

"That really ticked me off. I stayed. And from then on, every time something didn't work, I spoke up. I realized that you can make a difference if you speak up and set your mind to changing things."

Sumner Redstone
Chairman and CEO of Viacom

Follow your own instincts, not those of people who see the world differently.

"In my business career, I frequently turn to Ace Greenberg of Bear Stearns. I've known him for well over 15 years. In connection with all the transactions in which I have been involved, starting with the Paramount acquisition, Ace was one of my advisors. He has consistently advised me that you must follow your own instincts, rather than the views of naysayers or others who see the world in a different way.

"I put that advice into practice with Viacom. I had a terrific battle—most people forget it—a really vicious battle with Terry Elks for Viacom. People said at the time that I overpaid. They said MTV was a fad. They said Nickelodeon would never make it. I knew so little at that time about our businesses. But I saw MTV not as just a music channel but as a cultural channel, a generational channel, and a channel that could travel around the world. As for Nickelodeon, my instincts as a parent and as a grandparent told me, What's more important to people than a kids' channel? My instincts also told me that children are pretty much the same all over the world. They have the same issues with their parents, with their teachers. Everyone said I overpaid. My investment was $500 million. And even at the low price of our stock today, my stock is worth many, many billions. And that is a great illustration of why Ace's advice has been so valuable."

Meg Whitman
CEO and President of eBay

Be nice, do your best—and, most important, keep it in perspective.

"Several pieces of advice I've gotten in my life have really made a difference.

"'Be nice to people.' This sounds like a platitude, but I'll never forget my father telling me that. I was 10, and I had been mean to someone. He said, 'There is no point in being mean to anyone at any time. You never know who you're going to meet later in life. And by the way, you don't change anything by being mean. Usually you don't get anywhere.'

"Remember that you can do anything you want to do. Don't let anyone say, 'You're not smart enough ... it's too hard ... it's a dumb idea ... no one has done that before ... girls don't do that.' My mom gave me that advice in 1973. And it allowed me to never worry about what others were saying about my career direction.

"'Always do the best job you can do at whatever you're assigned, even if you think it's boring.' Jerry Parkinson, an assistant advertising manager and my boss at P&G, told me this in 1979. Here I was fresh out of Harvard Business School, and I was assigned to determine how big the hole in the Ivory shampoo bottle should be: three-eighths of an inch or one-eighth of an inch. I did research, focus groups ... and I would come home at night wondering how I had gone from HBS to this. But later I realized that any job you're given is an opportunity to prove yourself.

"'Don't be a credit hog. If you're constantly in the neighborhood of good things, good things will happen to you.' Tom Tierney, who was my boss at Bain in 1981 and is now on the eBay board, told me this. It's true—you get ahead by crediting other people.

"Finally, in 1998, I was in New York watching the ticker as eBay went public. My husband is a neurosurgeon. I called into his operating room and told him the great news. And he said, 'That's nice. But Meg, remember that it's not brain surgery.'"

Jack Welch
Former chairman and CEO of General Electric

Be yourself.

"It was 1979 or 1980. I was on the board of GE for the first time. And I was in Seattle for one of those three-day director outings. I had just gone to my first or second board meeting, and at a party for the directors afterwards, Paul Austin, the former chairman of Coke, came up to me. He was a reserved, formal man. Anyway, he must have noticed my starched shirt and how quiet I was in the meeting. I was all prim and proper. He said to me, 'Jack, don't forget who you are and how you got here.' I gave him an embarrassed 'thanks.' But I knew what he meant. I had always been myself except in this instance. I had never been quiet. He hit me in the nose with it, and it was startling. Next meeting, I think I spoke up a bit."

Sallie Krawcheck
CFO of Citigroup

Don't listen to the naysayers.

"When I was a kid, I was 'that kid' —freckles, braces, and very unfortunate glasses. If I wasn't the last chosen for the team, I was the second to last. There are so many heartbreaking stories I remember, like the time I finally managed to kick the ball in kickball. I was running for first base all excited, and then my glasses fell off and I had to go back and get them. The teasing was really tough. I wasn't just crying in class; I was falling apart at school. My grades went from A's to C's.

"One day when I was really down, my mom sat me on the sofa. She spoke to me as though she was speaking to another adult, telling me to stop paying attention to the girls who were teasing me. She told me that they were naysayers who would sit on the sidelines and criticize those who were out there trying. She said that the reason they were doing it was because they were jealous. Looking back, I know they weren't really jealous, but, at the time, I believed my mom. My grades went back up, and I never let the naysayers bother me again."

Vivek Paul
President and CEO of Wipro Technologies

Don't limit yourself by past expectations.

"The best advice I ever got was from an elephant trainer in the jungle outside Bangalore. I was doing a hike through the jungle as a tourist. I saw these large elephants tethered to a small stake. I asked him, 'How can you keep such a large elephant tied to such a small stake?' He said, 'When the elephants are small, they try to pull out the stake, and they fail. When they grow large, they never try to pull out the stake again.' That parable reminds me that we have to go for what we think we're fully capable of, not limit ourselves by what we've been in the past. When I took over Wipro in 1999, we were the first to articulate that an Indian company could be in the global top ten [of technology services firms]. As of 2004, we were.

> *"The best advice I ever got was from an elephant trainer near Bangalore."*
> —VIVEK PAUL

"The second-best piece of advice was something I learned from Jack Welch on one of his trips to India. He was commenting that every time he lands in New York he imagines that he's just been appointed chairman and that this is his first day in the role, and the guy before him was a real dud. He said, 'Every time, I think, What would I do that was different than the guy before? What big changes would I make?' I took that seriously. You should always think, 'How do I regenerate myself?' I don't do it religiously every time I fly internationally. But over Christmas break time, I set aside a day to zero-base myself. I force myself to do it every single year.

"But the person I rely on most in terms of advice is somebody in my Young President's Organization group: John Donahoe [former managing partner at Bain & Co., now president of the eBay business unit]. John has been a life coach for me, helping me sort out the many conflicting business and personal priorities. He has given me great advice about raising high school kids. His suggestions are invaluable."

Dick Parsons
Chairman and CEO of Time Warner

When you negotiate, leave a little something on the table.

"The best business advice I ever received was from Steve Ross, who used to run this company. Steve was a friend. It was 1991 or 1992, and I was on the Time Warner board. I was going to be coming over to the company from the banking industry, and we were talking about how to get things done. Steve said to me, 'Dick, always remember this is a small business and a long life. You are going to see all these guys come around and around again, so how you treat them on each individual transaction is going to make an impression in the long haul. When you do deals, leave a little something to make everyone happy instead of trying to grab every nickel off the table.'

> *"Steve said, 'Remember that this is a small business and a long life.'"*
>
> —DICK PARSONS

"I've used that advice a thousand times since, literally. When I got to this company, for the first seven or eight years I was here I was the principal dealmaker, and I always took that advice with me into a negotiation. Most people in business do not follow that, though. Maybe there was a time when they did, but I don't think most people do now. I think people get hung up with their advisors, investment bankers, lawyers, and others, and every instance becomes a tug of war to see who can out-duel the other to get the slightest little advantage on a transaction. But people don't keep in mind that the advisors are going to move on to the next deal, while you and I are going to have to see each other again."

Andy Grove
Chairman of Intel

When "everyone knows" something to be true, nobody knows nothin'.

"The best advice I ever got was from Alois Xavier Schmidt, my favorite professor at the City College of New York. A saying of his stayed with me and continued to influence me as the decades unfolded. He often said, 'When everybody knows that something is so, it means that nobody knows nothin'.'

"Our little research group at Fairchild [Semiconductor] some 40 years ago started to study the characteristics of surface layers that were the heart of modern integrated circuits. At that time, 'everybody knew' that surface states, an artifice of quantum mechanics, would interfere with us building such chips. As it turns out, nobody knew nothin': We never found any surface states; what we found was trace contamination. When we identified and removed this, the road opened up to the chip industry as we know it today.

"I remembered Professor Schmidt's words again ten years ago, when I was diagnosed with prostate cancer. 'Everybody knew' what treatment would be best for me. I thought that perhaps this was another case where common wisdom might be suspect and decided to do my own research, comparing all the known data about various treatment outcomes and coming up with less-than-conventional conclusions. Time and again, Professor Schmidt's saying prompted me to think for myself, go back to first principles, and base knowledge on facts and analysis rather than on what 'everybody knew.'"

Anne Mulcahy
CEO of Xerox

Remember the parable of the cow in the ditch.

"One piece of advice I got has become a mantra at Xerox. It came from a very funny source. It was four years ago, and I was doing a customer breakfast in Dallas. We had invited a set of business leaders there. One was a plainspoken, self-made, streetwise guy [Albert C. Black Jr., president and CEO of On-Target Supplies & Logistics, a logistics management firm]. He came up to me and gave me this advice, and I have wound up using it constantly. 'When everything gets really complicated and you feel overwhelmed,' he told me, 'think about it this way: You gotta do three things. First, get the cow out of the ditch. Second, find out how the cow got into the ditch. Third, make sure you do whatever it takes so the cow doesn't go into the ditch again.'

"Now, every time I talk about the turnaround at Xerox, I start with the cow in the ditch. The first thing is survival. The second thing is, figure out what happened. Learn from those lessons and make sure you've put a plan in place to recognize the signs, and never get there again. This has become sort of a catchphrase for the leadership team. It's just one of those incredibly simple commonsense stories to keep people grounded. I bet that businessman had no idea what kind of legs his story would have."

Brian Grazer
Academy Award-winning movie and TV producer,
Imagine Entertainment

All you really own are ideas and the confidence to write them down.

"I've spent the last 18 years soliciting advice from people outside the movie business. Before that, I sought advice from people in the enter-

> *"I've collected advice from close to 1,000 people over 30 years."*
> —BRIAN GRAZER

tainment industry. So I've collected advice from close to 1,000 people over 30 years. Every month I create a new list of people to call. I call it my 'interesting people list.' I call, on average, five people a week—I'll personally call Eliot Spitzer or Isaac Asimov—and may end up meeting with one every two weeks. Ideally I like to meet these people in my office. And I ask them to tell me about their world. I meet these people to learn ultimately how to be a more efficient filmmaker.

"My whole career has been built on one piece of advice that came from two people: [MCA founder] Jules Stein and [former MCA chairman] Lew Wasserman. In 1975 I was a law clerk at Warner Bros. I'd spent about a year trying to get a meeting with these two men. Finally they let me in to see them. They both said, separately, 'In order for you to be in the entertainment business, you have to have leverage. Since you have none—no money, no pedigree, no valuable relationships—you must have creative leverage. That exists only in your mind. So you need to write—put what's in your mind on paper. Then you'll own a piece of paper. That's leverage.'

"With that advice, I wrote the story that became *Splash*, which was a fantasy that I had about meeting a mermaid. For years, I sent registered letters to myself—movie concepts and other ideas—so that I had my ideas officially on paper. I have about 1,000 letters in a vault. To this day, I feel that my real power is only that—ideas and the confidence to write them down."

Rick Warren

Minister, founder of Saddleback Church and
author of *The Purpose-Driven Life*

Regularly sit at the feet of Peter Drucker.

"In life you need mentors, and you need models. Models are the people you want to emulate. I recommend that your models be dead. I'm serious. You don't know how people are going to finish up. A lot of people start out like bottle rockets. They look great, but then the last half of their life is chaos. That can be quite devastating.

"In my life, I've had at least three mentors: my father, Billy Graham, and Peter Drucker. They each taught me different things. Peter Drucker taught me about competence. I met him about 25 years ago. I was invited to a small seminar of CEOs, and Peter was there. As a young kid—I was about 25—I began to call him up, write him, go see him. I still go sit at the feet of Peter Drucker on a regular basis. I could give you 100 one-liners that Peter has honed into me. One of them is that there's a difference between effectiveness and efficiency. Efficiency is doing things right, and effectiveness is doing the right thing. A lot of churches—not just churches, but businesses and other organizations—are efficient, but they are not effective.

"Another important thing that Peter has taught me is that results are always on the outside of your organization, not on the inside. Most people, when they're in a company, or in a church, or in an organization, they think, 'Oh, we're not doing well, we need to restructure.' They make internal changes. But the truth is, all the growth is on the outside from people who are not using your product, not listening to your message, and not using your services."

> *"I recommend that your models be dead."*
> —RICK WARREN

Jim Collins
Author of the bestseller *Good to Great*

___

The real discipline comes in saying no to the wrong opportunities.

"It was 1994. [My book] *Built to Last* had just come out. I mean, I was nobody. But a colleague knew Peter Drucker, and one day I got a message on my voicemail: 'This is Peter Drucker. I would be very pleased to meet you for a day in Claremont [Calif., where Drucker lived].' I call back, very nervous, and he says, 'Speak up! I'm not young anymore!' So I'm like, 'PETER DRUCKER, THIS IS JIM COLLINS!' And then he actually set aside a day. Think about the value of a day with Peter Drucker at age 85. The interesting thing is that he absolutely changed my life that day. In one day.

"I was at a point where I could have started a consulting firm, Built to Last Consulting, or something. The first thing he asked was, 'Why are you driven to do this [start a consulting firm]?' I said I was driven by curiosity and impact. And he says, 'Ah, now you're getting in the realm of the existential. You must be crassly commercial.'

"For a moment I had this image of going to Yoda for wisdom, and having him say, 'Have a Coke!' But he was either testing me, or it was a joke. I'm not sure which.

"The huge thing he said to me was, 'Do you want to build ideas to last, or do you want to build an organization to last?'

"I said I wanted to build ideas to last.

"He said, 'Then you must not build an organization.'

"His point was, the moment you have an organization, you have a beast to feed-this army of people. If you ever start developing ideas to feed the beast rather than having ideas that the beast feeds, your influence will go down, even if your commercial success goes up. Because there's a huge difference between teaching an idea and selling an idea. In the end, what are you in a battle for? You're battling to influence the thinking of powerful, discerning people. If you ever abuse that trust, you can lose them. So the moment that arrow changes direction, you're dead.

"He said something else important: 'The real discipline comes in saying no to the wrong opportunities.' Growth is easy. Saying no is hard.

"I'll never forget asking, 'How can I ever pay you back?' and his saying, 'You've already paid me back. I've learned so much from our conversation.' That's when I realized where Drucker's greatness lay, that unlike a lot of people, he was not driven to say something. He was driven to learn something.

"I feel proud that I followed the advice. It's a huge debt. I can never pay it back. The only thing I can do is give it to others. Drucker had said, 'Go out and make yourself useful.' That's how you pay Peter Drucker back. To do for other people what Peter Drucker did for me."

Peter Drucker
Business consultant

Get good—or get out.

"The most important instruction I received was when I was just 20 and three weeks into my first real job as a foreign affairs and business editor of the large-circulation afternoon paper in Frankfurt. I brought my first two editorials to the editor-in-chief, a German. He took one look at them and threw them back at me saying, 'They are no good at all.' After I'd been on the job for three weeks, he called me in and said, 'Drucker, if you don't improve radically in the next three weeks, you'd better look for another job.'

"For me, that was the right treatment. He did not try to mentor me. The idea would have been considered absurd. The idea of mentoring was post–World War II. In those days [before World War II] you were hired to do your job, and if you didn't do it, you were out. It was very simple."

> *"If you didn't do your job, you were out. It was very simple."*
>
> —PETER DRUCKER

Ted Turner
Founder of CNN and former vice chairman of Time Warner

Start young.

"The best advice I ever got came from my father. He told me to go to work at his billboard company when I was 12 years old. I worked 42 hours a week, just like an adult. I worked the first summer as a water boy, a runner, and an assistant to the construction crew. Over the next 12 summers, I worked in a different area every year. I learned sales and leasing. I could paint billboards. I can post bills. My father would explain how the business world works—how a good business depends on good labor relations, enthusiastic leadership, making a profit, and reinvesting it. When I was 21 and went to work in the company full-time, I was ready. He passed away three years later, when I was 24, and I was able to take it over without a hitch. People couldn't believe how successful I was. This turned out to be the best business course I could have gotten."

David Neeleman
CEO of JetBlue

Balance your work with your family.

"I'm a God-fearing guy. And the best advice I ever got came from the head of our [Mormon] church, Gordon B. Hinkley. It was when we were going public in 2001, and I was caught up in the money, power, and glory. He cut me right down to size. In a conference where he was speaking, he reminded me, 'It's all about your family, your relationships. You've got to balance that with your work.'

> *"I was caught up in the power, money, and glory. He cut me right down to size."*
>
> —DAVID NEELEMAN

"So I set rules to be with my family and to keep everyone from encroaching on my time. I keep weekends as free as humanly possible. I try to make it home in time for nightly Scripture study and prayer as a family, and I try to make sure to take some good vacations when my kids are out of school. Those rules have had a positive effect on the business. I've seen so many people who have neglected their families. Now their kids are giving them trouble, so they're distracted. If you have a closer family, you can be a lot more focused when you're at work."

Mickey Drexler
CEO of J. Crew

Bail out of a business that isn't growing.

"It was 1980. I had been working at a department store [Bloomingdale's] for 12 years, and I knew I had to get out. There wasn't really a future there for me. I was offered the job of president at Ann Taylor [the women's-wear chain, a division of a now defunct corporation called Garfinckel Brooks Brothers Miller & Rhoads]. I thought about it—and when you are changing jobs, you think of all the reasons you should not do it. Then you get a little nervous. I said no.

"That night I was having dinner with someone who was older and wiser, Arthur Levitt [then chairman of the American Stock Exchange], and I told him about the offer. He said, 'I would grab that position at Ann Taylor. Department stores are a non-growth business.'

"He was right. The next morning I told the corporation I was interested after all. I resigned the next week. That was by far the best advice I've gotten in my life. If I didn't have dinner with him that night, I don't think I would have called back and said I wanted the job. And I am not sure I'd be where I am today."

Brian Roberts
CEO of Comcast

Let others take the credit.

"My mentor is my father, Ralph, who turns 85 this month. When I wanted to start my Comcast career at corporate headquarters, my father wisely insisted that I learn the business from the field, even though that isn't the way he started. One of my first summer jobs in college was as a cable installer in New Kensington, Pa., near Pittsburgh. I struggled to climb the telephone poles, strung cable, and went into people's homes to wire them. I really learned the ropes from people at the system level. That experience drove home how important our technicians and customer service representatives are, and how dangerous some of those jobs are at times. That empathy and understanding was something Ralph knew couldn't be taught in corporate headquarters.

"Ralph is a great listener. He doesn't feel the need to direct the conversation. Usually, when you come in, there's the problem and then there's the real problem; there's the agenda, and there's the hidden agenda. Just by listening and asking questions, he lets you get to the heart of the issue that you are chewing on. He's not looking to take credit for anybody's work. In fact, the single best piece of advice Ralph ever gave me was to let others take the credit. 'You're in a lucky position, and you know it,' he told me. 'You don't need all the glory. If you let others take the credit, it makes them feel like they're part of something special.' He's right. That's just the way Ralph is with me, and that's the way I try to be with others."

Marc Benioff
Founder and CEO of Salesforce.com

Incorporate philanthropy into your corporate structure.

"I was on a panel about business and philanthropy at a conference in 2001. Alan Hassenfeld, who at that time was CEO [now chairman] of Hasbro, took me aside afterward and told me I had a lot of good ideas, but I had to give them more structure. He said I should also incorporate the ideas of volunteerism [into Salesforce.com]. To meet somebody who had already fully integrated something like this into his company was critical. Hasbro has one of the richest philanthropic programs of any U.S. commercial organization. One of the many things they do is make toy donations to children's hospitals. It wasn't something Hasbro did by writing a check; it was part of their culture.

"We ended up putting 1 percent of our equity into the nonprofit Salesforce.com Foundation, as well as 1 percent of our profits, which of course at the time were zero. But following Alan's advice, we also put in 1 percent of our employees' time. That's six days a year of company-paid time for volunteerism. Employees want to work for us because of these programs -they want to reach out and do volunteerism anyway, and we give them a structure. Also, we let nonprofits use our service for free. Alan's advice ended up being really important, because this is what sets Salesforce.com apart from being just another company."

Hector Ruiz
CEO of AMD

Surround yourself with people of integrity, and get out of their way.

"In my adult years as a manager, Bob Galvin, the former CEO of Motorola, was my most influential leader. He told me, 'A good leader knows he is doing a good job when he knows with certainty that he can say yes to anything his staff asks and feel totally confident that they will do the right thing.' If you surround yourself with the right people who have integrity, and they all understand well the goals and objectives of the organization, then the best thing to do as a leader is to get out of their way. I use this advice quite a bit at work. The right people will feel far more pressure to perform well when they are trusted.

"I was given another piece of wisdom that has made a huge difference. When I was at Texas Instruments [from 1972 to 1977], my boss's boss, Al Stein, who was running the semiconductor business, one day asked me, 'What's the worst thing that could happen if you make a decision that doesn't work out?' I remember thinking, 'I guess I could get fired.' I realized that in the scheme of things, that seems so insignificant. It was almost like an epiphany."

Donny Deutsch
CEO of Deutsch Inc. and host of
CNBC's *The Big Idea With Donny Deutsch*

If you love something, the money will come.

"Back in 1983 I went to work as an account executive at my dad's ad agency, David Deutsch Associates. I was a fuckup from the beginning. I was supposed to be taking care of clients, but I was 24 years old, still partying, not ready to grow up. And he fired me. My dad said, 'You know, you're not passionate about what you are doing here. So get the fuck out of here! You don't love this, and I don't want you around here, because I love what I do.' Then he said, 'Look, whatever you do in life, find something you love-I don't care if you're a garbage man-and everything else will fall into place. If you love something, you'll be great at it, and the money will come and everything else will fall into place.'

"It was hard to take. But he knew I needed a kick in the ass, and I did. So what else could I do? I cleaned out my desk, and I went out to the West Coast. I kicked around, went on *Match Game* [a TV game show] and won $5,000. Then I came back East, sold jeans in a flea market. I thought about law school. In the process, I found myself.

"Six months passed, and I found out my dad was thinking about selling the business. He had an offer, for not a lot of money, but it would have allowed him to stay on for a few years after the deal closed. He was in his mid-50s. So this was what he wanted. And I said to him—I don't know how, in hindsight, I had the balls or stupidity to do this—I said, 'Don't sell it. I want to come back. I just don't

> *"My dad said, 'You're not passionate about this. So get out of here!'"*
> —DONNY DEUTSCH

want to be an account guy. But put me in a corner and leave me alone. I'll work on new business. Just let me build my own little thing here.'

"From that point on, I went to the wall. I started pitching new business instead of holding clients' hands. As luck would have it, I had a real skill for it, and I loved it. Seven years later I became CEO, my dad retired happily to become a painter, and we're now one of the ten largest ad agencies in the country."

Klaus Kleinfeld
CEO of Siemens

Keenly visualize the future.

"The best advice I ever got was from an old friend of the family's, and it goes like this: Whenever you take on a new position, before you jump in and get bogged down in the details, sit down, lean back, close your eyes, and think about what you really want to achieve and how you want things to look in a couple of years. And only then—once you have a clear vision in front of your inner eye—start executing so that things will move in that direction. I was in my early 20s at the time, and the family friend, Georg Brandl, was probably in his mid-80s. He had been born in Bavaria, and after receiving a manual education as a construction worker, he went on to lead large construction projects around the world.

"When I was working as a consultant on many restructuring projects, this was always the approach I took with the core leadership team. Even though we couldn't see any end state because there were so many problems in front of us, I would put that aside and say, 'Okay, what should this look like?' It always started with me as a personal thing—thinking it through and then drawing people in.

"I was never able to tell Georg Brandl how helpful that advice has been."

> *"I would put aside problems and say, What should this look like?"*
> —KLAUS KLEINFELD

Ann Fudge
Chairman and CEO of Young & Rubicam Brands

___

Don't chart your career path too soon.

"It was 1978—oh, God, that seems so long ago. I was a year out of Harvard Business School. I was working at General Mills as a marketing assistant on Cheerios. One day I was having a conversation with the product manager on Cheerios, Kent Tippy. He was complaining about how MBAs want to be CEOs and measure how fast they make it to this level and that level. In fact, one guy in our group was keeping score—he had people's careers all charted out. I admit I was looking ahead too. I really wanted to be a product manager. Kent said to me, 'Don't look too far ahead. Focus on what you're doing right now.' He convinced me that people who are good in product management tend to be good executors but may not have the skills to go to higher levels of leadership. So it's not useful to chart your career path so early on. You're better off demonstrating capabilities at each level—to do X, Y, and Z when you're asked to do X. Following his advice, I really tried to excel in each job. It worked."

Herb Kelleher
Founder and chairman of Southwest Airlines

___

Respect people for who they are, not for what their titles are.

"I'd say my mother made more of a difference to me than anyone else did. I know that's a conventional and perhaps mundane answer, but my family was blown apart at the start of World War II. We went from six to two people, my mother and myself.

"There were so many things I learned from her. One piece of advice that always stuck in my mind is that people should be respected and trusted as people, not because of their position or title. Frequently, position or title did not reflect the true merits of a person. I got a lesson confirming that almost immediately, because there was a gentle-man [in our town] who was the head of a financial institution. He was always dressed immaculately, and he gave the impression of being a very upstanding guy. Well, he was indicted, convicted, and sent to jail for embezzling

"Thanks to her advice, in the business world I try not to judge any-one by superficial standards. I try to approach them with an open mind. I'm very interested in their ideas. You don't have to have a doc-torate to have an idea. You ought to be open to listening to people. Show that you care about them as individuals, not just as workers. You know how some people are always looking over your shoulder to see if there's somebody more important behind you? Well, one of the things that I've tried to do—If I'm talking to a person, that person is the only person in the world while we're talking. They're owed that. Besides, they're usually fascinating. Getting together with the people of Southwest is one of the most rewarding and exciting things in my business life."

Clayton Christensen
Harvard Business School professor

You can learn from anyone.

"Kent Bowen was my partner in a company we started in Boston before I switched to academia. He was a professor at MIT then. If they ever give a Nobel Prize in material sciences, he should get it. Once I realized he was the best in his field, I asked him, 'How does it feel to be the top guy in the world in your field?' Without denying my character-ization of him, he said: 'You know, there's a real disappointment.' He said something like, 'When I was younger, I looked up at the top of the mountain and thought, Wow, those guys are really smart! When you're near the top of the mountain looking down, you think, Boy, if nobody is smarter than I am, the world is really hurting.'

"That had such a profound impact on me. I realized that a lot of us, when we're in school, believe that you can learn only from people who are smarter than you. But if you move toward the top of that hill and maintain that belief, then your opportunities for learning become progressively more constricted. So what you need is a fundamental humility—the belief that you can learn from anyone."

Ted Koppel
Former anchor of ABC's *Nightline*

Do what you love.

"There was a very famous radio reporter in New York City in the 1950s, '60s, and '70s. His name was Danny Meenan, and he was the quintessential old Irish reporter. I was about 22, just out of graduate school, and had gone to work at WMCA, where Danny worked, with the exalted title of copy boy. Being a copy boy meant you did what anybody else on the staff wanted you to do. Danny was a very generous mentor. He knew I wanted to be a reporter. He took me on a couple of assignments with him.

"Shortly thereafter, he and I repaired to a bar and had a couple of beers together, and Danny said, 'What do you want to do with your life?' I said, 'I think I want to go into politics. I might want to be a Congressman someday.' He looked at me as if I had just said or done something obscene. He said, 'You would be a lousy Congressman.

> *"He looked at me as if I had just said or done something obscene."*
> —TED KOPPEL

And it looks as though you are going to be a pretty good reporter. You will have much more fun being a reporter than being a Congressman. And you should do what you're good at, and do what you love. And you look to me that you are loving journalism.'

"It's what I've been doing for the last 40 years."

FOLLOW THESE LEADERS

By Christopher Tkaczyk; Matthew Boyle

Carley Roney

The Knot co-founder and editor-in-chief since 1996

Leading is like parenting:
It's one long process of pulling back.

On letting go: When I had my first child, I worked through the whole thing—I was home for maybe three weeks. The second time around, I just couldn't do that. What's funny about it is that I had to rely on my true leadership skills rather than just putting in the time. I trust my staff, and leaving at 6:30 when I know they are staying until 9:30 is an example of that trust. You just have to let go. Leading a company is like parenting: It's one long process of pulling back and letting it become its own organism. You have to make sure you have created an organization that is able to operate with or without you.

On swallowing pride: The great balance of leadership is to have fervor over what you believe, but not be afraid to admit when you are totally wrong. I'll convince my staff about the hot trends of the season. Then I'll go to two more fashion shows and find out that I'm totally wrong. You have to be willing to swallow your pride, but as long as you care most about your product, you don't mind.

Favorite leader: Vaclav Havel, the first President of the Czech Republic. He made people believe that they could achieve their own destiny. —M.B

Terry Lundgren
Federated CEO since 2003

"I listen, but shortly after, the second piece is to pull the trigger."

On not noodling: I have always been a pretty good listener, and I am quick to admit that I do not have all the answers. So I am going to listen. But shortly after I listen, the second piece is to pull the trigger. I have all the input, and here is what we are going to do. People need closure on a decision. If you listen and then noodle on it, people get confused, and that's not effective leadership.

On driving change: When I was 35, I became CEO of Bullocks Wilshire, a division of Federated. The person I replaced had just retired and there was not a lot of change going on in the organization. I knew that we were not attracting young consumers, so we decided to try some new things in advertising. We had done line-drawn ads for 50 years, and it wasn't working. But it was the heritage of the company. The response was mutiny—"How could you come in here and do that?" I didn't know if it was right, but you have to have good instincts in this business. I brought in someone to change the marketing, and all of a sudden we saw a contemporary point of view.

Favorite leader: Martin Luther King Jr. With all the odds against him, he took a stand for what he believed in.—M.B

Kevin Sharer
Amgen CEO since 2000

"As a leader you are putting your ass on the line. You should be scared."

On leadership school: In the Navy I had 80 people working for me on a nuclear submarine in my early 20s, so that was on-the-job leadership training of the highest order. Then, at General Electric working on Jack Welch's staff, I got a chance to see him at his peak. For a thirtysomething, that was learning at the feet of the master. I remember sitting in the audience at a meeting where Jack said GE would be the No. 1 market-cap company in the world. This was at a time when IBM seemed untouchable. I thought to myself, "I don't know if that was brave or fanciful or delusional, but I will sign up for that."

On what all successful leaders share: Courage. You are trying to engender a passion and a desire to do something new. And new is scary. As a leader, you are putting your ass on the line to make it happen. So you should be scared.

On feedback: You have to get ongoing constructive feedback to push you out of your comfort zone. This is never more important than when you are CEO. My direct reports go off every year and write my performance review. I also write each executive a two-page letter over Christmas that summarizes their performance and what I want them to focus on next year.

On whether it's better to be loved or feared: I think it's better to be trusted. Fear kills candor and guarantees that the organization will perform below its potential. And the problem with being loved as a single element is that it does not mean they respect you.
Favorite leader: Admiral Lord Nelson. As a leader of engagement, he taught every lesson that I know. —M.B

Carol Bartz
Autodesk CEO from 1992 to 2006

*"Taking yourself too seriously
is the worst thing you can do."*

On people watching: I think leadership is something that comes naturally. But you can keep fine-tuning a style. The way I do it is by watching people. I love watching people's good and bad attributes and saying, "Gee, that makes a lot of sense for me." I'm not a big fan of mentoring, because that is like trying to match up two snowflakes.

On what leaders need: If you're not excited, how can you get others excited? People will know. It's like how kids and dogs can sense when people don't like them.

On the biggest mistake: Taking yourself too seriously is the worst thing you can do. I have a sense of humor, but there have been times when I also take myself too seriously. That's especially true with new leaders. They're in the spotlight and feel as if they always need to have the right answer to protect their image. But, really, you just have to be proud of who you are naturally.

Favorite leader: Bill Clinton. When you are introduced to him, it's as if you are the only person in the room. —M.B

Stanley O'Neal
Merrill Lynch CEO since 2003

---

*"Look for integrity. I think this is
a bedrock requirement."*

On teamwork: Surround yourself with the very best people, and spend a lot of time trying to create a common sense of purpose—a mission—and an environment in which people can have an opportunity to realize their full potential. I've been fortunate at Merrill in that, over 19 years, I have had exposure to virtually every part of our firm. So I've been able to meet all of the individuals who today make up my top-tier team. I think that there's no substitute for that depth of knowledge.

On finding future leaders: Look for integrity. I think this is a bedrock requirement. Beyond that, it's clarity of thought. How a person attacks a problem or an opportunity is often more important than the conclusion he comes to, because it tells you something about how this individual is going to face other situations.

Loved or feared? No right-thinking person wants to be feared. Fear is a negative emotion. It is one that inhibits performance. Who wants to be feared? I think the better word is "respected."

Favorite leader: Martin Luther King Jr. I grew up in the 1950s and 1960s in the segregated South. I'm sure he had doubts. And like every human being, he had fear. But he did not let that overtake him. —C.T.

Bill Zollars
Yellow Roadway CEO since 1999

"I was about to get my kneecaps shot off, and I had no clue."

On leading abroad: I spent eight years working overseas. Working with Europeans when you are the only American in that group gives you more empathy and more humility and a much broader perspective. Your success is based on how well you work as a team. I saw others who tried to lead through command and control and failed. People like to think of Europe as one place, but it isn't. To go over there and to tell people what to do resulted in disaster.

On knowing the landscape: When I was at Kodak in the 1980s, we were buying up photofinishers in Europe to create a network to sell film to. It was a great strategy that someone in Rochester thought up. But in Italy it wasn't working. So one day the Italian general manager and I go out to dinner in Milan, and he says, "Bill, this strategy will not work in Italy." I said, "I know it's difficult, but we have to." He says, "You don't understand. In Italy, photofinishing is a family business." I said, "I understand, it's the same as everywhere else." He said, "Bill, I don't mean a family business. I mean the family business." He was talking about the Mafia. Here I was about to get my kneecaps shot off, and I had no clue. I learned that before you launch off on something, you should take the time to understand what you're getting yourself into.

On communicating: Visibility is incredibly important. It's very hard to lead through e-mails. When I first got to Yellow, we were in a bad state. So I spent 85 percent of my time on the road talking to people one-on-one or in small groups. I would start off in the morning with the sales force, then talk to drivers, and then the people on the docks. At the end of the day I would have a customer dinner. I would say the same thing to every group and repeat it ad nauseam. The people traveling with me were ready to shoot me. But you have to be relentless in terms of your message.

On leading vs. managing: Managing is making sure that you are doing things right. Leading is making sure that you are doing the right things.

On failing fast: A leader has to get across the idea of "failing fast." Don't be afraid to try things, but if something doesn't work, move on. What people sometimes try to do is prove they were right in the first place.

Favorite leader: Harry Truman. He was a no-nonsense type of guy. He did not parse his words and followed through on what he said he would do. That's very unusual for a politician. —M.B

Hank Paulson
Goldman Sachs CEO from 1998 to 2006

"I start by talking about some of the mistakes I've made."

On humility: I started work at Goldman Sachs in 1974, watching people who were successful and people who weren't. And the things that make a good leader are being open-minded, having a willingness to really ask for and accept advice, showing a sense of humility, and putting the right people in the right seats.

On leading 20,000 people: Culture is key. This year I taught 26 sessions on accountability and leadership—six hours each—for our 1,200 managing directors all over the world. I start these sessions by talking about some of the mistakes I've made and that the company has made. The 300 partners get together for two-day retreats. Every year I speak at the orientation for all new analysts and associates in the firm. What we do in terms of communication is unusual for a company of 20,000 people.

On criticism: One of the things we have done for years is 360-degree reviews. It's amazing when you go to a leader and say, "There are 30 people who reviewed you, and 30 of them trust you. But all 30 say you don't listen well." It has an impact.

Favorite leader: China's former Premier Zhu Rong-ji. I respect anyone who can manage change the way he did. —C.T.

Brad Anderson

Best Buy CEO since 2002

"Over the years I've developed more stubbornness."

On having a vision: When I first started at Sound of Music [the precursor to Best Buy], it was basically on the verge of bankruptcy. [Longtime CEO] Dick Schultz was obsessed with talking about this $50 million company we were building. As a manager, I couldn't see that. All I saw were obstacles. I thought he was not connected to reality. But he had the vision. I'm probably still a bit of a rebel, so I admire leaders with a point of view that is not conventionally held.

On sermons: I went to seminary school for a year and dropped out quickly. But when I was there, one of the professors said to us, "If you have one good sermon in you, you're lucky." When you have a strong point of view, you become confident and passionate about it. Over the years I've developed more stubbornness.

Favorite leadership book: The Bible. It shows how to deal with all sorts of people, from oligarchs to dissident, angry people.

On what works for him: I'm most effective with one-on-one coaching. I would guess I coach 100 to 200 employees in a given month. I don't really think you can do the kind of leadership I do on a formal basis. It has to be genuine. I don't think you can force a human connection. Favorite leader: The first President Bush. I admire his capability and balance as a leader. —M.B

Paul Tagliabue
NFL Commissioner from 1989 to 2006

———

*"The future doesn't just happen
—it's shaped by decisions."*

On leading 32 team owners: When you are trying to persuade them to adopt a course of action, you don't try to change their minds as much as you try to show that it serves their own interests. I read a great book years ago about the Supreme Court that said the court's challenge was "to remember the future and imagine the past." That's a great phrase, because it says so much. You imagine the past in order to make it relevant to the future that you are creating. The future doesn't just happen—it's shaped by decisions.

On his biggest challenge: It was the decision in 1992 to agree to free agency and the salary cap as the new framework for our players. The owners had been operating for 70 years on the belief that the sport could never be successful with [free agency]. They thought the best players would gravitate to a few places and the big markets would have advantages. There was a critical point where a clear majority of owners felt we should keep slogging away in court, but myself and a few others thought that was wrong. So we just turned the minority position into the majority position. Looking back, it turned out to be the right thing to do.

Favorite leader: Winston Churchill. He had the willingness to go against the current, and he also had a great capacity to learn from the past. —M.B